Praise for Lee Edwards's previous books

Bringing Justice to the People:
The Story of the Freedom-Based Public Interest Law Movement

"This is the dramatic and never-before-told history of how Ed Meese and his freedom-based colleagues are successfully defending the Constitution and battling liberal litigators like the ACLU who would deny the fundamental rights of everyday Americans."

—Sean Hannity

"*Bringing Justice to the People* is the remarkable and readable story of a national legal movement committed to granting God a place in the public square, giving parents greater choice in their children's education, and allowing organizations like the Boy Scouts to stand up for traditional moral values. A must read for those who love freedom and the U.S. Constitution as originally written."

—Rush Limbaugh

Our Times: The Washington Times 1982–2002

"This fascinating collection of essays should be compulsory reading for all conservative who wish to remind themselves of what conservatism has done for the world. As such, *Our Times* is a fine tribute to a great newspaper. I hope and trust that the *Washington Times* will go from strength to strength."

—Margaret Thatcher

The Conservative Revolution:
The Movement That Changed America

"This is an important book. Unlike many other writers and historians, Lee Edwards takes seriously the thought, the battles, and the accomplishments of twentieth-century conservatism."

—William J. Bennett

"Here is the story of conservatism's progress from the fringe to the center of American politics, told by someone who lived the story."

—George F. Will

"Lee Edwards's fast-paced and engaging account of a half-century of American conservatism is a contribution to righting the balance.... Edwards truly does have a lot to crow about. Conservatives will love this book, and liberals can learn something from it."

—*Washington Post*

"Veteran conservative activist and author Lee Edwards has provided a timely and useful history of the rise and growth of the conservative movement in the second half of the 20th century."

—*Human Events*

The Power of Ideas: The Heritage Foundation at 25 Years

"Edwards does a thorough and workmanlike job of chronicling a body that has guided Republican thinking from Ronald Reagan to Newt Gingrich."
—*New York Times Book Review*

Goldwater: The Man Who Made a Revolution

"... is not an unfriendly account ... but it is an informative and brutally honest one, required reading for anyone who pretends to understand this political giant and perplexing enigma."

—*Arizona Republic*

Missionary for Freedom: The Life and Times of Walter Judd

"... few will be left unmoved after reading this engrossing political biography of a man who made an indelible imprint on history."

—*Booklist*

The Essential
R o n a l d
REAGAN

A Profile in Courage, Justice, and Wisdom

Lee Edwards

ROWMAN & LITTLEFIELD PUBLISHERS, INC.
Lanham • Boulder • New York • Toronto • Oxford

ROWMAN & LITTLEFIELD PUBLISHERS, INC.

Published in the United States of America
by Rowman & Littlefield Publishers, Inc.
A wholly owned subsidary of The Rowman & Littlefield Publishing Group, Inc.
4501 Forbes Boulevard, Suite 200, Lanham, Maryland 20706
www.rowmanlittlefield.com

PO Box 317
Oxford
OX2 9RU, UK

Distributed by National Book Network

British Library Cataloguing in Publication Information Available

Library of Congress Cataloging-in-Publication Data

Edwards, Lee.
  The esential Ronald Regan : a profile in courage, justice, and wisdom / lLee Edwards
    p. cm.
  Includes bibliographical references and index
  ISBN 0-7425-4375-7 (Cloth : alk. paper)
  1. Reagan, Ronald. 2. United States—Politics and government—1981–1989.
  3. Presidents—United States—Biography. I. Title.
  E877.E77 2004
  973.927'092—dc22   2004017760

Printed in the United States of America

⊗™ The paper used in this publication meets the minimum requirements of
American National Standard for Information Sciences—Permanence of Paper
for Printed Library Materials, ANSI/NISO Z39.48–1992.

To Anne

Also by Lee Edwards

Bringing Justice to the People: The History of the Freedom-Based Public Interest Law Movement (editor)

Educating for Liberty: The First Half-Century of the Intercollegiate Studies Institute

Mediapolitik: How the Mass Media Have Transformed World Politics

Our Times: The Washington Times 1982–2002 (editor)

The Conservative Revolution: The Movement That Remade America

The Global Economy: Changing Politics, Society, and Family (editor)

Freedom's College: The History of Grove City College

The Collapse of Communism (editor)

The Power of Ideas: The Heritage Foundation at Twenty-five

Goldwater: The Man Who Made a Revolution

Missionary for Freedom: The Life and Times of Walter Judd

John Paul II in the Nation's Capital (editor)

Rebel Peddler

You Can Make the Difference (with Anne Edwards)

Ronald Reagan: A Political Biography

Contents

Preface

I N THE EARLY AFTERNOON OF JUNE 5, 2004, Ronald Wilson Reagan quietly "slipped the surly bonds of earth" and touched the face of God.[1] The death of any president is momentous, but the passing of President Reagan from Alzheimer's disease at the age of ninety-three evoked seven days of national remembrance, sorrow, and affection not seen since the assassination of John F. Kennedy in November 1963 and the wartime death of Franklin Delano Roosevelt in April 1945.

Reagan's death was his last great gift to America. It inspired almost everyone to lay aside controversies like the war on terrorism and the state of the economy and pause to remember his unquenchable optimism and his principled leadership. In death, as in life, Ronald Reagan appealed to the best in the American people.

Here is what some said about his legacy. "We know his greatness as a president by what we don't see today," said his authorized biographer Edmund Morris. "Where is the Soviet Union? Where is the double-digit inflation? Where is the welfare population? Where is the national malaise?"[2] "Reagan will be remembered," remarked the late historian Stephen Ambrose, "as the president who reversed the decades-old flow of power to Washington."[3]

"On foreign policy," said Senator Edward M. Kennedy, "he will be honored as the president who won the Cold War."[4] "Ronald Reagan got it right," wrote economist Lawrence Lindsey, a former member of Reagan's Council of Economic Advisers. "Now, just about every country is pursuing the three pillars of Reaganomics: lower taxes, sound money and less regulation."[5]

While they were speaking, the body of Ronald Reagan made a stately week-long journey across America, starting at a funeral home in Santa

Monica, California, festooned with flags and flowers and signs that read "God Bless the Gipper," and then taken by hearse to the Reagan Presidential Library in Simi Valley. Uniformed firefighters standing on a bridge raised a large American flag and saluted the procession passing beneath them. At the library, more than 100,000 paid their respects to the late president, bringing with them wreaths, memorial cards, and jars of jellybeans, Reagan's favorite candy.

Not everyone sang his praises. The Reagan legacy, Nobel Prize economist James Tobin said, was "a crippled federal government."[6] Reagan "showed a clear hostility to civil rights aspirations," charged Jack Greenberg, former counsel for the NAACP Legal Defense and Educational Fund.[7]

Regarding Reagan role's in the Iran-contra affair, historian C. Vann Woodward said he knew of "nothing comparable with this magnitude of irresponsibility and incompetence."[8] "Reagan was one of the most despicable presidents," the gay political activist Robert Kunst said, "responsible for 500,000 American AIDS deaths and 10 million worldwide, while he catered to the right wing in this country."[9]

Television news mixed moving pictures of the late president and the memorial services with sometimes acerbic comments about his legacy. U.S. efforts to deal with the tough issues in the Middle East "went on hold" during the Reagan years, said CBS's Bill Plante, helping to "set the stage for the first Iraq war and the rise of Islamic fundamentalism." At the end of his presidency, stated ABC's Peter Jennings, " a great many people thought he'd made the wealthy wealthier and had not improved life particularly for the middle class." "I don't think history has any reason to be kind to him," said CBS's Morley Safer on CNN's *Larry King Live*.[10]

But the majority of eulogists chose to emphasize what they regarded as the blessings that had flowed from his presidency. Mikhail Gorbachev, the former Soviet leader who had participated in four summit meetings with Reagan, said the American president "made a huge, possibly decisive, contribution to creating conditions for ending the Cold War."[11] Lady Margaret Thatcher, the former British prime minister who had been Reagan's strongest supporter among European leaders, said that he "achieved the most difficult of all political tasks: changing attitudes and perceptions about what is possible."[12]

Reagan accomplished that daunting task, wrote foreign policy analyst David Ignatius, because he was able "to mobilize moralism and pragmatism in a way that eventually toppled the Soviet Union."[13] And he did it because he was a great presidential communicator, said one observer, "one of the three greatest to hold the office—Abraham Lincoln, master of the written speech; Roosevelt, master of the radio address; and Reagan, master of television."[14]

Again and again a comparison was made between two seemingly disparate political leaders—Franklin D. Roosevelt and Ronald Reagan. After FDR's death in 1945, wrote presidential historian Michael Beschloss, the *New York Times* predicted that "men will thank God on their knees a hundred years from now" that Roosevelt had been the president to fight Hitler and Tojo. "It is not too much to suggest," said Beschloss, that with Reagan's death, Americans might give similar thanks that they twice elected a president who "saw the chance to end the Cold War in his own time."[15]

In the nation's capital Reagan's body was slowly carried up Constitution Avenue in a horse-drawn black caisson, followed by a riderless horse, to the Rotunda of the U.S. Capitol where the 700-pound casket was placed upon a pine-board catafalque built for Abraham Lincoln's coffin in 1865. More than 100,000 people from nearby and far away waited in line for as long as six hours to honor the man about whom biographer Lou Cannon wrote, "The greatness of Reagan was not that he was in America, but that America was in him."[16]

Driven as if by some elemental urge, political analysts could not stop talking about the fortieth president and the changes he had wrought. He transformed the conservative movement, wrote columnist David Brooks, "from a past- and loss-oriented movement to a future—and possibility-oriented one." He was "the Moses of the conservative movement," said political analyst Marshall Wittmann.[17]

He was, they said, a true son of the Midwest. "He really had the brand of small-town, Midwest America stamped on him," said Richard Norton Smith, former director of the Reagan Presidential Library. He earned his optimism the old fashioned way, they said—through adversity. "He was someone," wrote Reagan speechwriter Peter Robinson, "who understood how to take the bad in life and find good in it."[18]

And while they were talking, his casket was brought to the gothic-columned Washington National Cathedral for a state funeral attended by four former presidents—Gerald Ford, Jimmy Carter, George H. W. Bush, and Bill Clinton—25 heads of state, and 180 ambassadors and foreign ministers. The U.S. Marine Corps Chamber Orchestra offered Bach, and Irish tenor Ronan Tynan sweetly sang Schubert's "Ave Maria." Justice Sandra Day O'Connor, appointed by Reagan to be the first woman on the U.S. Supreme Court, read from John Winthrop's 1630 sermon to fellow Pilgrims aboard the *Arabella* bound for the Massachusetts Bay Colony. "We shall be as a city upon a hill," O'Connor read—one of Reagan's favorite images—[and] "the eyes of all people are upon us"—one of Reagan's strongest beliefs.

There were eulogies by Thatcher, who remarked that "we have one beacon to guide us that Ronald Reagan never had; we have his example;" by former president and vice president George Herbert Walker Bush, who, his voice breaking, said, "I learned more from Ronald Reagan than from anyone I encountered in all my years of public life"; and from President George W. Bush, who said, "Ronald Reagan belongs to the ages now [echoing what had been said about Lincoln], but we preferred it when he belonged to us."

There were also those who were happy to see him go. "He who never should have been born has died," broadcast Radio Reloj, Communist Cuba's official radio station. Some feigned indifference like the AFL-CIO, which kept its Washington headquarters open on the national day of mourning to make the point that the former president was "a union-buster" (a reference to his decisive action against the air controllers' illegal strike in the first months of his presidency). Others spoke grudgingly like Jimmy Carter, who remarked, "I think throughout his term in office, he was obviously very worthy of the moniker that was put on him, that is, the Great Communicator."[20]

And there were those who tried to explain why he had been so important to them. Michael Schaedler drove eleven hours from Augusta, Maine, to join the line of mourners winding up Capitol Hill and into the Rotunda where Reagan lay in state. "I was a drug addict," he admitted. When he tried to kick the habit, he wrote President Reagan and the president responded—surprising and inspiring Schaedler, clean for thirteen years and now a counselor to other recovering addicts.[21] A cross-country trip to a city where he has no family or friends was no deterrent for Derace Owens of Jacksonville, Texas. "Reagan never put himself first," he said, tears filling his eyes, "The least we can do is . . . put him first."[22] Conceding it was a "sad event," Kathleen Briggs of Williamsburg, Virginia, said that it "has brought the country together again."[23]

At the end of a long day and a long week, Ronald Reagan's body was returned to California for a sunset burial service at the Reagan Presidential Library where the three Reagan children spoke fondly about their father, sharing childhood memories and describing him as a man with a deep faith—"My father never feared death," said Patti; "he never saw it as an ending"—and then, following a soulful playing of taps by an army bugler, Ron, Patti, and Michael gently led their grieving mother Nancy still whispering "I love you" away from the casket.[24]

After all the millions of words and pictures—Ronald Reagan was the most photographed and filmed president in American history, and the television networks used every available image during their saturation coverage of the memorial week—after all the opinions and judgments: "Where does Ronald Reagan stand in the long line of American history?" asked political historian Michael Barone. "He occupies," he said, "the place in the second half of the twentieth century that Franklin Roosevelt held in the first."[25]—We are left with the essential question: How did this one man— a former film and television actor whose most commercially successful movie starred a chimpanzee, an unabashed political conservative who insisted that government was the problem not the solution, and that communism should be defeated not contained, the acknowledged successor to a conservative Republican who lost a presidential election by the largest popular margin in U.S. history—change not only a nation but the world?

Let us begin not at the beginning but at a turning point in Ronald Reagan's first serious quest for the presidency.

A Time of Testing

NOTHING SEEMED TO BE WORKING for presidential candidate Ronald Reagan, something the former film star and two-term California governor was not used to. It was the early spring of 1976, and he had lost five straight Republican primaries to President Gerald Ford. His campaign was nearly $2 million in debt. The polls were depressing. Most of the party professionals, including every living chairman of the Republican National Committee but one, had written him off. The media, including his hometown paper, the *Los Angeles Times*, were saying he ought to be realistic and concede. His campaign staff was at the end of their tether—unbeknownst to him, his director John Sears was secretly talking to the Ford camp about the ways and means of a graceful exit. Nancy was convinced her husband would only "embarrass" himself if he kept campaigning and losing.[1]

Downcast conservatives were wondering if political lightning was about to strike their champion as it had Robert A. Taft in 1952 and Barry Goldwater in 1964. As editor of *Conservative Digest*, I was planning a Republican National Convention issue with the Reagans on the cover and an exclusive interview with the candidate titled, "My First One Hundred Days as President." Would I have to abandon the idea?

Reagan's old friend and campaign chairman, Nevada senator Paul Laxalt, left a gloomy Washington headquarters and flew to Raleigh, North Carolina, expecting to meet a candidate as despondent as his staff. Instead, Laxalt encountered a determined, combative Reagan with his back up because of all the demands that he get out. "I'm taking this to the convention in Kansas City," a steely-eyed Reagan vowed, "and I'm going even if I lose every damn primary between now and then."[2] But Reagan, ever the optimist, believed he could still win the presidential nomination.

I

The hard-core conservatives running his North Carolina campaign—Senator Jesse Helms and state chairman Tom Ellis—agreed, but only if Reagan abandoned his speak-no-ill-of-your-opponent strategy and went after the president hard, particularly on his accommodationist foreign policy. And they knew which specific issue would galvanize their people—the proposed give-away of the Panama Canal. In the Florida primary, Reagan had brought conservatives roaring to their feet when he said of the canal, "We built it, we paid for it, it's ours, and we're going to keep it!" He described Panamanian general Omar Torrijos, who was demanding the return of the canal, as a "tinpot dictator."[3]

Reagan had videotaped a half-hour talk explaining why the United States should not surrender the canal ("One of the most effective speeches of his political career," his press secretary Lyn Nofziger thought), but time and money had run out before it could be shown in Florida.[4] Ellis obtained a copy of the video and determined to air it in prime time on fifteen television stations throughout North Carolina at a total cost of only $10,000 (the price of two thirty-second TV spots in New York City). At the same time, Reagan, along with Nancy and his longtime Hollywood friend Jimmy Stewart, visited every major city and more than a few minor ones in the state. An unbounded Reagan never let up on Ford, challenging his policies in Cuba, Angola, and Panama, criticizing his budget deficits, and saying that if he had been president he would have warmly welcomed Alexander Solzhenitsyn, the famed survivor and chronicler of the Gulag Archipelago, to the White House.

The year before, the Ford White House had at first explained that "scheduling problems" prevented a visit by the Russian dissident and then suggested clumsily that Solzhenitsyn was in the United States "to promote his books" and the president did not want to endorse the Russian author's "commercial purposes."[5] Conservatives knew the real reason for the rebuff was that Secretary of State Henry Kissinger believed that America was a modern Athens and Soviet Russia a modern Sparta and that given America's weakened position following the fall of South Vietnam to the Communists, détente was the only "realistic" foreign policy for the United States. Kissinger had warned President Ford that seeing Solzhenitsyn would damage U.S.-Soviet relations and set back détente. Reagan dismissed such *realpolitik*.

In North Carolina, Reagan carried the fight directly to the president, declaring that Ford would be vulnerable on a host of issues in the November election. He asked Republicans how they would answer the Democrats when they pointed out that Ford had "presided over the greatest budget deficits in the nation's history." How would Republicans defend themselves against the Democrats in the area of foreign policy, Reagan asked, when America under President Ford had become "second in military strength in a world where it is fatal to be second best?" How could Republicans campaign for change in Washington, he asked, for a reduction in the bureaucracy and a cutback in regulations restricting freedom and competition "when these things have all gotten worse in the past nineteen months?" Looking out at his Republican audience, the usually self-effacing Reagan said that he would not be asking for their support if "I didn't believe in my heart I offered us the best opportunity for victory next November."[6]

Conservative author M. Stanton Evans has correctly described the March 23, 1976, Republican primary in the Tarheel State as "the second most important primary in modern conservative politics"—the first being the epic Goldwater-Rockefeller California primary in June 1964.[7] Failure in North Carolina would have sounded a death knell for Reagan's nomination hopes—and any immediate prospect of the conservative movement becoming a major political force in America because Ronald Reagan and American conservatism were joined as surely as Siamese twins. Rejected by the voters yet again, Reagan would have been unable to conduct an effective nomination campaign with little money, a dispirited organization, and reporters constantly asking, "Governor, when are you going to withdraw?" After a token appearance at the National Republican Convention, Ronald Reagan would have returned home to California and political obscurity, just one more promising politician who never fulfilled his promise. And a forlorn conservative movement would have cast about for another national leader, always looking back at what might have been under Reagan.

But Ronald Reagan stunned Jerry Ford and most political observers by winning the North Carolina Republican primary by 54 percent to 46 percent and capturing a majority of the delegates. He achieved a political resurrection and went on to pose the most serious challenge to an incumbent Republican president since Theodore Roosevelt took on William Howard Taft six decades earlier. Conservatives all over the country were rejuvenated, and I happily proceeded with my special convention issue starring "President" Reagan.

Several factors accounted for Reagan's upset victory, such as the planned U.S. giveaway of the Panama Canal and a maladroit Ford speech in which he talked so condescendingly about women as homemakers that even women who were proud to be homemakers wanted to break a rolling pin over the president's head. Reagan's energetic campaigning and the fervent support of the Helms organization also made a difference. Helms, then in his first term as a U.S. senator, personally toured more than thirty Carolina counties in a three-day blitz leading up to primary day. Conservative organizations such as the American Conservative Union supplied crucial manpower and money. Also, voters began viewing Reagan as "an underdog fighting the entire Republican establishment," and no one loves an underdog more than the American voter.

Undergirding all these things was the candidate's Lincolnesque trust in the people. "A president has got to take the truth to the people," Reagan told me that spring when I interviewed him at his Pacific Palisades home overlooking Los Angeles, "tell the people what he is trying to accomplish, what's standing in the way, and then depend on the people" to help him succeed.[8] But the single most important factor that made the difference between victory and defeat was the thirty-minute TV speech. A poll of Republican voters revealed that 20 percent of them made up their minds in the last week of the campaign, and among them, three out of four went for Reagan.[9]

In the pivotal North Carolina primary, Ronald Reagan exhibited the essential characteristics that defined him all his political life—the physical stamina and mental toughness to keep going when everyone else was ready to give up, the ability to articulate core issues in clear concise language, the courage to take a principled position in the face of conventional wisdom, a willingness to trust in the informed judgment of the people, and a God-centered serenity that things will turn out for the best.

For such a man, challenging an incumbent president did not seem an impossible task. Indeed, he had been taught from an early age that all things were possible for him who believed.

CHAPTER I

From the Heartland

Tiny Tampico, Illinois, is 788 miles from Washington, D.C. In the early 1900s, it was a cozy town of about one thousand people with the usual Midwestern mix of stores, schools, churches, two lumberyards, an "opera" house, a park with a seventeen-foot memorial topped by a Union soldier, and a small railway used mainly for shipping by neighboring farmers. "No one was rich in Tampico, but no one starved or went without shoes in winter."[1] The residents were, for the most part, hard working, patriotic, and comfortable with their small-town life, benefiting from the general prosperity of pre–World War I America.

It was there on February 6, 1911, during the presidency of Republican William Howard Taft, that Ronald Wilson Reagan was born in a small apartment above the bank building. His brother John Neil (Moon) had been born two years earlier. As the new baby boy bawled, his father remarked, "For such a little bit of a fat Dutchman, he makes a hell of a lot of noise, doesn't he?"[2] "Dutch" quickly became Ronald Reagan's nickname in the family and among his friends. The ironic remark was typical of the new father, John Edward (Jack) Reagan, quick-witted and quick-tempered. Jack Reagan was nearly six feet tall, muscular, and swarthy with thick, wavy, brown hair, and a captivating storyteller. He was Irish Catholic—the Reagans had come from Ireland to Illinois before the Civil War—but an indifferent churchgoer. Ambitious and seemingly destined for a successful career as a salesman, Jack was too fond of alcohol, prone to weekend benders that often lasted into Monday.

The new mother provided a clear contrast. Nelle Clyde Reagan was small and slender with light brown hair and blue eyes. Gentle and soft-spoken, she was Protestant (a member of the Disciples of Christ, known today as the Christian Church), deeply religious, and a teetotaler. But she took pains to impart a sympathetic understanding of her husband's alcoholism to her two sons, telling them not to turn against their father—his drinking, she explained, was "a sickness he could not help."[3] Her generosity of spirit made a deep impression on Dutch, whose early life centered around his mother who made her younger son her special charge.

Dutch was eleven years old when for the first time he came home to find his father flat on his back on the front porch and drunk. "Seeing his arms spread out as if he were crucified," he later wrote, "I could feel no resentment against him."[4] The slender boy managed to drag Jack Reagan inside and put him to bed. Different Reagan biographers have explored what it means to be the child of an alcoholic—keeping your feelings to themselves, lying when it would be easy to tell the truth, cautious about intimate relationships.

But Lou Cannon of the *Washington Post,* who covered candidate, governor, and president Reagan for twenty-five years, makes the essential point that Ronald Reagan was the *successful* child of an alcoholic. Such resilient children, according to a prominent psychiatrist, have a positive self-image, a caring attitude, and a belief in the importance of self-help, all characteristics of Ronald Reagan, young and old.[5] Unlike many adult children who flee from their alcoholic parents, Reagan brought Jack and Nelle to California to live with him shortly after he became a film actor. He cared for them to the end of their lives.

The Reagans were Democrats, Jack making it a point to vote straight Democratic. A fierce individualist, Jack Reagan believed, with the Declaration of Independence, that all men were created equally. Dutch recalled that when the racist film *The Birth of a Nation* came to town, "my brother and I were the only kids not to see it." Explained their father, "It deals with the Ku Klux Klan against the colored folks, and I'm damned if anyone in this family will go see it."[6] Once, when he was on the road, Jack was told by a hotel clerk, "We don't permit a Jew in the place." Jack immediately walked out, telling the clerk, "I'm a Catholic, and if it's come to a point where you won't take Jews, you won't take Catholics."[7] Jack Reagan never completed grade school; Nelle did but went no further. But both were avid readers and their home was always filled with books and magazines. Nelle taught Dutch to read by the age of five by sitting with him every night and having him follow her finger as she read the newspaper. In later years, she and her two boys would sit at the kitchen table while she read aloud uplifting stories about King Arthur and the Round Table and the Three Musketeers.[8] "Looking back," Reagan said, his mother's reading and his own left in him "an abiding belief in the triumph of good over evil."[9]

Nelle's sole recreation, outside her family and church, was to offer dramatic readings of melodramas like *East Lynne* before the local ladies society with "the zest of a frustrated actress."[10] She sometimes enlisted her reluctant young son in her presentations although Dutch was more interested in touchdowns than curtain calls. According to biographer Paul Kengor, Nelle was well known for her recitations, self-written stories and poems that dealt not only with God but with other themes such as democracy, and on at least one occasion the boyhood of George Washington— "surely a story that must have made an impression on young Dutch."[11]

Jack Reagan was "in" shoes, working variously as a shoe clerk, the manager of a shoe department, and part owner of a shoe store. But he never made more than $35 a week, success being denied him because of bad investments and an inability to control his drinking. The wandering Reagans lived in a number of small Illinois towns west of Chicago as well as in the Windy City itself before finally putting down roots in Dixon in December 1920 where Dutch lived until he was past twenty-one. "The Reagan family really didn't know where the next buck was coming from," Neil Reagan wrote me. "But Nelle always had the right outlook on life and was sure that 'before the next payment was due, God would find a way.'"[12] In Chicago, Jack Reagan's salary was so modest the family lived in a flat lighted by a gas jet that provided light only if you put a quarter in the hall meter. Nelle made all the clothes for the two boys. Nevertheless, Dutch adopted his mother's firm belief that there was a God-given purpose in everything that happened—good or bad. "I've always believed," he said, "that we were, each of us, put here for a reason."[13]

As the twenties began, Americans had high hopes for themselves and the future. Republican Warren G. Harding had won the presidency, easily defeating Democratic governor Edward C. Cox (and his young running mate, Franklin D. Roosevelt). The handsome easy-going Harding insisted that "America's present need is not heroics but healing; not nostrums but normalcy; not revolution but restoration."[14] But what was normalcy in America—national Prohibition or gin-soaked cities? The emancipation of women or the continuing lynching of African Americans? The national adulation of aviator Charles Lindbergh or the crowded revival meetings of evangelist Billy Sunday? Stock market bulls or bears?

Such questions did not trouble the inhabitants of Dixon, a bustling town of about eight thousand built on gently rolling northern Illinois hills and containing several plants and factories. The town courthouse faced the venerable Nachusa Tavern that had extended its hospitality to such celebrities as Abraham Lincoln and General Ulysses S. Grant. Other important landmarks were the Family Theater, a small but well-stocked public library, and North High School for which Dutch Reagan passionately desired to play football.

When Dutch entered high school, he was only five feet three inches tall and weighed 108 pounds, a more apt candidate for water boy than lineman. But he persisted because of its physical challenge and because his bad eyesight (he was obliged to wear huge black-rimmed spectacles) would not be a handicap. Baseball was impossible—"when I stood at the plate," Reagan wrote in his early autobiography, "the ball appeared out of nowhere about two feet in front of me." There was no invisible ball in football, he noted with relief, "just another guy to grab or knock down."[15] By the middle of his junior year, he had filled out dramatically and, never missing a practice, became a regular 165-pound right guard.

Dutch was a voracious reader and a frequenter of the Dixon public library located only five blocks from the Reagan's small white-framed house. From about the age of ten, he checked out an average of two books a week, mostly boys' adventure stories such as Edgar Rice Burroughs's Tarzan stories and Burt L. Standish's Frank Merriwell series, but also the Western novels of Zane Grey and the works of Mark Twain. "The library," he wrote years later, "was really my house of magic."[16] He was an eye-learner rather than an ear-learner, showing an early aptitude for retaining what he read. At age twelve, Dutch read *That Printer of Udell's: A Story of the Middle West* by the popular novelist Harold Bell Wright, later admitting to his official biographer Edmund Morris that the book made him "a practical Christian."[17]

The novel is a remarkable foretelling of the future. The hero is Dick Walker, whose mother is a committed Christian with an alcoholic husband. Her dying words—actually the first words in the novel—are "O God, take ker o' Dick!" Young Dick travels to Boyd City, an industrial Midwestern city, but is unable to secure a job until George Udell, a devout

Christian, hires him as a printer. Thus begins a Horatio Alger ascent to personal and spiritual fulfillment. Dick Walker is a natural orator who persuades the citizens to sponsor a workfare program for the needy rather than "haphazard, sentimental" welfare. As he puts it in a pivotal scene, "As I understand it, the problem that we have to consider is, briefly, how to apply Christ's teachings in our own city."[18] A grateful citizenry decides to send Walker to "a field of wider usefulness," and the novel ends with Dick kneeling in the snow before setting out with his new wife for Washington, D.C. to represent Boyd City in Congress. Immediately after reading *That Printer of Udell's*, Dutch told his mother, "I want to be like that man."[19] His first step was to be baptized and welcomed on June 21, 1922, into the First Christian Church, whose fundamentalist beliefs included the infallibility of the Bible, the virgin birth of Jesus, the Resurrection, and the Second Coming.

Reagan remembered Christmas as "special" because of his mother and "her joyous spirit about the day . . . she made sure we knew the meaning of Christmas." The Reagans could not afford decorated trees, but Nelle used ribbon and crepe paper to decorate a table or "create a cardboard fireplace out of a packing box."[20] On many holidays, the Reagans visited the Wilsons (Dutch's aunt and uncle), and it was at their farm that the youngest Reagan encountered a new invention that significantly shaped his life. "I remember sitting with a dozen others in a little room with breathless attention," he later wrote, "a pair of earphones attached tightly to my head, scratching a crystal with a wire." He heard a faint voice saying, "This is KDKA Pittsburgh, KDKA Pittsburgh."[21] There is an apocryphal story that Dutch Reagan stood and imitated the announcer, winning laughter and persuading him to repeat the performance.[22] But Reagan does not mention any such encore in his two autobiographies.

Following Nelle, Dutch had the lead in several school plays and in the opinion of his brother Moon was very good, a judgment shared by the faculty adviser to the dramatic club. He found time to teach his own Sunday school class to a group of attentive boys. Interviewing Reagan's pupils sixty years later, biographer Norman Wymbs was startled to discover that they remembered specific lessons Dutch had taught.[23] He capped his high school career by being elected president of the student body. "He was a natural leader," his social science teacher and mentor Bernard J. Frazer wrote me, who had a quality "that not too many high school kids had—he did what he started."[24] And he was an unflagging optimist as reflected in a poem he wrote for the high school yearbook *The Dixonian*:

> I wonder what it's all about, and why
> We suffer so, when little things go wrong?
> We make our life a struggle
> When life should be a song.[25]

During the summers, Dutch worked. When he was fourteen he was a construction worker at thirty-five cents an hour on a ten-hour-a-day, six-days-a-week schedule. He spent most of his time swinging a pick at heavy blue clay. He did it but understandably did not like it, once dropping his pick in the middle of a downward stroke when the noon lunch whistle blew. But the long hours in the open air added muscle to his slender frame and enhanced his chances of making the football team.[26] In the summer of 1925, he made $200 but did not spend a dime of it—an early sign of the personal discipline he practiced all his life. "I knew it was for something else," he recalled, "college."[27] The next summer he got a job he was to keep for seven years—the sole lifeguard at Lowell Park, a recreation area on the fast-flowing Rock River. He received a salary of fifteen dollars a week, plus all the hamburgers, onions, pickles, and root beer he could consume at the food stand.

From 1926 through 1932, Dutch Reagan saved an impressive seventy-seven people from drowning—a figure the skeptical writer Garry Wills has documented as accurate. Six feet one inch tall and weighing a smoothly-muscled 175 pounds, Reagan was a handsome, self-confident youth who cheerfully worked twelve hours a day, seven days a week at Lowell Park. His one complaint was that people rarely thanked him or rewarded him when he saved their lives. "The only money I ever got," he remembered, "was ten dollars for diving for an old man's upper plate that he lost going down our slide."[28]

The twenties with their Republican control of the White House and Congress were a frustrating time for a loyal Democrat like Jack Reagan, who was galvanized in 1928, however, by the Democrats' nomination of New York Governor Al Smith for president. He plastered Al Smith banners all over his car and lauded the governor's sharp attacks on the Volstead Act. And he stressed to barroom listeners that Smith was the first Roman Catholic to run for president in American history. The Happy Warrior from New York carried all the big cities, but Republican Herbert Hoover received 58 percent of the popular vote and a decisive electoral majority of 357 because, historian Samuel Eliot Morison wrote, the average worker was working, the average businessman was doing good business and neither was interested in changing things. "You can't lick this Prosperity thing," Will Rogers said, "even the fellow that hasn't got any is all excited over the idea."[29]

Seventeen-year-old Dutch was too busy pulling people out of the water at Lowell Park to campaign for Smith, but he did join a protest march against outside workers being imported to work on local farms and in Dixon's factories. Asked years later to explain his initial political activism, Reagan replied, "In a small town you can't stand on the sidelines and let somebody else do what needs doing. . . . I felt I had to take a stand on all the controversial issues of the day."[30] His sense of social responsibility and rejection of bigotry were encouraged by both his father and mother. "I too have a dream," he wrote much later, "a dream that one day whatever is done to or for someone will be done neither because of or in spite of their race. We are all equal in the sight of God—we should be equal in the sight of man."[31]

Upon graduation from high school, Moon Reagan had gone to work for the Medusa Portland Cement Company (at $125 a month), but Dutch had his eye on Eureka College, which had about 250 students and was located some seventy miles south of Dixon. College was not the normal next step for a high school graduate in the late 1920s—less than ten percent of graduating seniors went on to a college or university. Furthermore, the economy was showing the stresses and strains that would erupt on Black Tuesday, October 29, 1929. Most parents of the time felt that college demanded four years that would be better occupied earning a living.

But Dutch was determined to enter Eureka because it had a good football team, it had been established by the Disciples of Christ—"Religious values shall be found in courses of study, in the work plan and in recreational activities," the catalogue declared—and because his high school sweetheart Margaret Cleaver had announced her intention to attend Eureka.[32] However, despite the summer savings he had so carefully accumulated, Dutch still did not have enough for the $180 tuition, plus room and board.

The prospective student traveled to Eureka and ardently argued his case before college officials who were impressed by his earnestness, the earnings from his summer jobs, and his athletic ability. They offered him a scholarship for his tuition and a dishwashing job for his meals—he would have to pay for his room. Dutch knew it would be hard going, but he was eager to test himself.

Down the Old Ox Road

Over the next four years, Dutch Reagan played a lot of football, joined a fraternity, won an acting award in a national play contest, was elected president of the student senate, majored in economics and sociology, and helped lead a successful student strike. And he wrote several revealing essays and autobiographical short stories, one of which ends with the young hero phoning his girl and saying to her, "This is the president." The reference is to the presidency of the student senate, but it is another intimation of the ambitions of the young man from the heart of Illinois who was anything but ordinary.

Dutch pledged Tau Kappa Epsilon (Teke), one of the prestigious national fraternities on campus. He became a reporter for the school paper, *The Pegasus*. With his ready smile and easy manner, he was tabbed a sure Big Man on Campus. It was almost inevitable that he should be picked as the freshman representative when Eureka students, for the first time in the school's history, went on strike.

The students were reacting to a decision by college president Burt Wilson to cut the curriculum as part of an economy program to "save" Eureka, which was experiencing mounting financial problems. The Wilson plan would have eliminated courses needed by many juniors and seniors to graduate, would have "decimated" the faculty, and would have seriously damaged the college's admittedly second-rate academic standing.[33] The student body, with the backing of most professors, submitted an alternative plan to the president who spurned it. The students then presented a petition to the college's board of trustees demanding that President Wilson resign.

Confident it would be rejected, Wilson offered his own resignation. When the trustees closed ranks behind their president at a late evening meeting, the college bell, by prearrangement, began tolling, calling the student body and faculty to the college chapel. There, freshman Dutch Reagan—dark-suited, white-shirted, and hair carefully parted in the middle—delivered a passionate speech urging a campus-wide strike. "When I came to actually presenting the motion," Reagan remembered, "there was no need for parliamentary procedure; they came to their feet with a roar—even the faculty members present voted by acclamation. It was heady wine."[34] It was Reagan's first experience with the power of words to move and motivate people politically. "With two more lines," he later speculated, "I could have had them riding through 'every Middlesex village and farm'—without horses yet."[35]

After one week—during which study hours were established and enforced, professors went to class and marked every absentee present, and a tea dance was held every afternoon—President Wilson's resignation was finally accepted by a narrow majority of the board of trustees. The strike ended, the faculty agreed to withhold any salary demands for the foreseeable future, and the school returned to normal, although ironically the trustees ultimately reduced the number of departments, a Wilson recommendation. Biographers Lou Cannon and Garry Wills assert that Reagan "misrepresented" some details of the strike—exactly when the midnight chapel meeting occurred, the strong animus between the president and the dean of the college—but there is no disputing the essential difference between what happened at Eureka and the "fevered picketing" on campuses during the 1960s: the outcome was decided democratically, not through threats and acts of violence.[36]

Ronald Reagan's singular ability to sense and reflect the feelings of the American people was first developed in a serious way during his years at Eureka College, a microcosm of Middle America in the late 1920s and early 1930s. In his first autobiography published thirty years later, Reagan presents a lyrical picture of these formative years (revealing his considerable talent as a writer):

> Oh, it was a small town, a small school, with small doings. It was in a poor time without money, without ceremony, with pleasant thoughts of the past to balance fears of the future.
>
> Those were the nights when we spent all of twenty cents on a date: two big cherry phosphates at the drug counter (with the big colored jars of water lighted up) and a walk home.
>
> Or when we danced in somebody's house or in the fraternity living rooms under the dimmest of lights, while the chaperones—always old Eureka grads who had met each other this way themselves—took a turn around outside or just dozed.
>
> Or when we devoured homemade cake and repressed heartburnings of a different sort as we strolled under the campus elms.

And there was the wonderful thing of inviting older people who knew some jokes and the ways of the world and how to talk to us without condescending; scrambling eggs before an open fire and talking about Hoover and his calm statements on prosperity; whipping up the hot chocolate and shaking our heads over this upstart Franklin D. Roosevelt, who was beginning to criticize from New York.[37]

And of course there was football. Still hampered by severe myopia, Dutch was a second string right guard until his junior year when he was moved up and averaged all but two minutes of every game for the rest of his college career. "Dutch was not an outstanding player," said football coach Ralph McKinzie candidly, "but he was a good plugger ... [with] a lot of spirit and desire."[38] He went out for the swimming team and wound up as captain. He tried out for track and won his letter in that sport as well. It was easy to keep in training because smoking was not allowed on campus and in the words of Neil Reagan (who quit the cement plant and followed his younger brother to Eureka) "the thought of having a drink was unheard of."[39] The training took: Ronald Reagan never smoked and (reinforced by his father's alcoholism) limited himself throughout his life to an occasional cocktail or glass of wine.

Eureka had no illusions about its academic prowess, middling at best, but it offered a classical liberal arts curriculum. In his freshman year, Dutch took courses in rhetoric, French, history, English literature, and math. Never a grind, he maintained a B average throughout his college years, aided by his photographic memory. The Eureka registrar later confirmed that he was "much above average in ability and accomplishments."[40] In between classes and sports, Dutch joined the campus dramatic society and enrolled in the dramatics course under Ellen Marie Johnson, who saw genuine talent in the tall handsome young man with the distinctive smoky-peat baritone voice.

The climax of Dutch's collegiate dramatic career came in his junior year when Johnson entered Eureka in the annual one-act play contest sponsored by Northwestern University. Only twelve colleges and universities were invited to present their productions out of hundreds of applicants—Eureka was the only school without a drama department to be included. Their play was Edna St. Vincent Millay's antiwar verse drama, *Aria da Capo*. Dutch Reagan played the Greek shepherd boy Thyrsis, who is strangled by a fellow shepherd. "No actor can ask for more," Reagan later wrote. "Dying is the way to live in the theater."[41]

To almost everyone's amazement, including the actors, Eureka finished second in the competition, and Dutch was one of three actors who received "Oscars" for his performance. The head of Northwestern's drama department asked the young Eureka star if he had ever considered the stage as a career. Acting was in fact Dutch's secret ambition, but America was in the early days of a depression and young Americans were expected to be practical about their future.

Asked decades later to name the single most important influence in his life, Reagan replied, "The Depression." It was the Depression that cost his father a partnership in a Dixon shoe store he had opened with borrowed money. It sent his mother to work in a dress shop for $14 a week. The income of the Reagan household was so meager that Dutch once sent $.50 home to his mother without his father's knowledge so the older Reagans could continue to shop at the grocery store.[42]

By the end of 1929, the whole economy was in decline. Every business was obliged to dismiss employees who, unable to find other jobs, defaulted on installment payments and used up their savings. The jobless turned to employed relatives or returned to a family farm, but the tailspin of the economy continued until mid-1932 when about 12 million people, 25 percent of the workforce, were unemployed.[43]

It was not the best of times for a young man to be setting out, but on a sun-bright, blue-skied day in June 1932—the same month that Franklin D. Roosevelt was nominated for president by the Democratic Party—Ronald Wilson Reagan graduated from Eureka College with a degree in economics and social science and letters in football, swimming, and track. He boasted to fraternity brothers, with far more confidence than he truly felt, "If I'm not making five thousand a year when I'm five years out of college, I'll consider these four years here were wasted."[44] Teacher and student agreed that Reagan was bound to succeed—but where? An old friend of the family asked him, "What do you think you'd like to do?" The young man had a ready answer, "Show business." The question was how to go about it. "Broadway and Hollywood," he later wrote, "were as inaccessible as outer space."[45]

CHAPTER 2

Going Hollywood

D
UTCH DECIDED TO TRY HIS LUCK in a part of show business where his voice would be an asset—radio—and as
an announcer about something he knew well—sports.
"He drove us nuts in the fraternity," Neil Reagan remembered, "as he
walked around broadcasting imaginary football games play by play."[1]

At the end of summer (after notching his seventy-seventh and final
"save" as a lifeguard), Reagan hitchhiked 130 miles to Chicago, the center
of American radio in the thirties. He had no contacts, no letters of introduction, and no experience, but lots of grit. He walked the city's hard pave-
ments for several days, visiting small and large stations like WGN. He got
nowhere except at NBC where a sympathetic woman in production told
him: This is the big time. You have to have experience. Get a job with one
of the smaller stations and then come back and see me.

Returning to Dixon, Dutch recounted his disappointing visit to his
father who offered him the family Oldsmobile to visit radio stations in the
general neighborhood. The following Monday Dutch made his first call at
WOC Davenport, Iowa, and asked to see the program director, who turned
out to be a vaudeville veteran named Peter MacArthur. "Where the hell have
ye been?" roared MacArthur in his Scottish burr. "Don't ye ever listen to the
radio?"

It seemed that WOC had been advertising for a staff announcer for a
month and had hired one out of ninety-five applicants the week before.
Dutch's temper flared and he stormed out, crying out as he did, "How in
hell does a guy ever get to be a sports announcer if he can't get inside a station?" He was waiting impatiently for the elevator when he heard a loud
voice echoing down the hallway. "Do ye perhaps know football?" asked a
scowling MacArthur. The would-be announcer replied that he had played

16

the game for eight years, and before he could say anything else was led into a vacant studio and told to describe a football game "and make me see it." The red lights flashed "on," and without any preparation, Dutch began describing from memory the fourth quarter of a game between Western State University and Eureka College the previous fall. Twenty minutes later, wringing wet from tension and determination, he ended his "broadcast" with "We return you now to our main studio."[2]

"Ye did great, ye big SOB," said a chuckling MacArthur, who hired him on the spot, offering him $5 a game and bus fare as a part-time announcer of the University of Iowa games. Dutch Reagan had convinced a thirty-year veteran he could handle the job—an impressive achievement for a twenty-one-year-old novice who had never stood before a real microphone before. But Reagan had been training for such an opportunity since his first reluctant participation in Nelle's dramatic readings before the ladies of Tampico and Dixon.

Within four months, WOC was incorporated into WHO in Des Moines, NBC's key station in the Midwest. Dutch Reagan became an Iowa and then a regional celebrity as WHO's leading sports announcer, and his salary went to $75 a week, plus bonuses and fees for appearances on the banquet circuit (usually lecturing on the virtues of temperance and clean living), writing an occasional column for the *Des Moines Register*, and handling announcing chores at public events when he was not broadcasting. He sent 10 percent of his salary to Moon to help him finish college and another 25 percent to Nelle to help pay the bills. Jack had had a serious heart attack and following a long convalescence was told he could no longer work.

Reagan's was not an automatic ascent. During his first year, he often made on-air mistakes and mispronounced words, triggering a bawling out by Pete MacArthur, who nevertheless recognized the potential in the young sports announcer who made it a point to be prepared, whatever the occasion. Directed to broadcast the Drake Relays, one of the most important amateur track events in the country, Reagan studied the history of past Drake Relays and memorized biographical material on former champions and present competitors. He was soon interviewing local politicians and national celebrities passing through Des Moines on personal appearance tours. As he did throughout his life, Reagan mixed the professional, the political, and the personal with an ease that masked his purposeful ambition and discipline.

Aware of his weakness with "first" readings, Reagan discovered that if he memorized the opening paragraph and repeated it out loud before he delivered it, "everything he read would sound spontaneous." The "natural" delivery came in fact from constant practice.[3] But it was the sound of his voice that made Ronald Reagan special as a sportscaster, actor, political candidate, governor, and president. It was a voice, wrote essayist Roger Rosenblatt, that "recedes at the right moments, turning mellow at points of intensity. When it wishes to be most persuasive, it hovers barely above a whisper so as to win you over by intimacy, if not by substance. . . . It was that voice that carried him out of Dixon and away from the Depression."[4]

Reagan remained a lifeguard even when no longer paid to rescue people; while swimming at Fort Dodge, he saved a girl from drowning. And shortly after his arrival in Des Moines, he also rescued a young woman from possible serious injury through a calculated bluff. Nursing student Melba Lohmann was walking to her hospital one Sunday evening when a man poked a gun in her back and demanded her purse. She then heard a voice coming from the window of a second-floor apartment above her: "Leave her alone, or I'll shoot you between the shoulders." It was Dutch Reagan, who came hurrying downstairs in his robe and pajamas holding a revolver. The would-be robber fled. Reagan, who walked Lohmann to the hospital, saw nothing remarkable in his feat. According to biographer Lou Cannon, he did not brag about what he had done or stay in touch with the young woman. Years later, as president, he admitted that his gun was not loaded, but, wrote Cannon, Reagan was "well armed with imagination, bravery, and a willingness to become involved in a situation where his own life could have been at risk. He was not passive in such moments."[5]

Republican congressman H. R. Gross of Iowa, who was a WHO newscaster in the 1930s, remembered Dutch Reagan as "an outstanding sports announcer—he was actually sports editor of the station—and very popular in the state of Iowa. I always thought he had very strong political possibilities. . . . He was conscientious, he had ability, he was honest and decent. What else can you say about a man?"[6] Republican Gross and Democrat Reagan would sharply debate national politics at lunch or in between broadcasts, a coworker remembered. Gross was "strongly opposed" to the New Deal, Dutch as strongly supportive. But over time, it seemed that "maybe Gross was winning Dutch over." The younger man still said he was a loyal Democrat and was still unreservedly enthusiastic about Roosevelt, a friend recalled, "but he had begun to talk about the government moving too heavily into peoples' lives."[7]

Reagan had warmly applauded the inspiring words of President Roosevelt when in his first inaugural address he asserted that "the only thing we have to fear is fear itself." Like most Americans, Reagan wanted a firm hand on the tiller of state, and he had responded positively to Roosevelt's First One Hundred Days when he shepherded thirteen major pieces of legislation through Congress, including insurance for all bank deposits, refinancing of home mortgages, Wall Street reforms, legalization of beer, and laws creating the National Recovery Administration and the Tennessee Valley Authority. What is not clear is whether Reagan understood how radical the New Deal was: it was writing a new contract between the government and the governed. Upon acceptance of the Democratic presidential nomination, Roosevelt had explained that the New Deal was not a political slogan but "a changed *concept* of the duty and responsibility of Government." Government, FDR declared, now "has a final responsibility for the well-being of its citizens."[8]

Reagan's primary responsibility was to his profession that he took seriously. He estimated that during his WHO years, he broadcast forty-five college football games from every "major press box in the Midwest," covered more than six hundred major league baseball games by telegraph (particularly those played by the Chicago Cubs), and handled swimming and track meets as well. He interviewed such sports personalities as Doc Kearns, Jack Dempsey's former manager, wrestler Ed (Strangler) Lewis, and heavyweight fighter Max Baer. He also met the English actor and Hollywood actor Leslie Howard at a fund-raising event for victims of an Ohio River flood and film star James Cagney on another occasion.

While in Des Moines, Dutch fulfilled one of his basic loves—horseback riding—by applying for a commission in the U.S. Cavalry Reserves. The opportunity to ride wonderful mounts and receive expert training in horsemanship was irresistible to Reagan, who says, "I think the Irish are one of the lost tribes of the Arabs." He completed his Army Extension courses with an overall average of 94 percent. An examiner found him to be in superb physical condition except for 20-200 vision in both eyes. Nevertheless, according to Edmund Morris, officer candidate Dutch Reagan satisfactorily drilled a war-strength mounted platoon at Fort Des Moines in a driving rain. On April 29, 1937, he was accepted into the

Reserve Corps as a second lieutenant with an "Excellent" rating for character and military efficiency.[9]

Welcoming the New Deal

Following Franklin D. Roosevelt's election in November 1932, Democratic loyalist Jack Reagan was rewarded with a federal job. He distributed food as well as government script which the needy poor used at the grocery. Like most of America, Dixon was hard hit by the Depression: the cement plant for which Moon had worked closed down, adding one thousand people to the already long list of unemployed. Jack spent much of his time finding and assigning jobs, rotating them so that every man would have at least a couple of days work.

But then welfare workers from back East arrived with files and furniture to begin bureaucratizing the process. "Government was busy at the job it does best," Ronald Reagan later remarked, "growing." The day came when Jack Reagan offered a week's work to some men who replied, "Jack, we can't take it." They explained that the last time they did so, the welfare office had cut off their relief. When they stopped working several days later, the men had to reapply for welfare. There were new interviews and new application forms to fill out. "The process took three weeks, and in the meantime their families went hungry—all because they'd done a few days' honest work."[10]

Next, Jack Reagan was appointed the local administrator of the Works Progress Administration (WPA). Under his direction, there were few boondoggles in Dixon, and he frequently came up with ingenious projects for able-bodied men. Once he figured out a way to use the old streetcar rails, torn from the main street, as structural steel in a hangar at the new airport. All the while, he battled the welfare bureaucrats who used every pretext including alleged physical unfitness to resist releasing their charges to the WPA. Jack shared his anger and frustration with his younger son who decades later as governor and then president would have his own battles with the bureaucracy.

But Dutch's enthusiasm for President Roosevelt and his criticism of former President Hoover continued unabated. During the 1936 election, he mentioned FDR on the radio whenever he could and perfected an imitation of Roosevelt's fireside chats that delighted coworkers. He insisted that

Herbert Hoover and the Republicans were responsible for the economic problems that continued to burden the Midwest and his family. And yet, the two men at station WHO who remained his lifelong friends and advisers were H. R. Gross and Voith Pemberthy, both staunch conservatives and Republicans.[11]

Most Americans agreed with Reagan's favorable view of the New Deal, and in the fall of 1936, President Roosevelt, aided by rises in wages and farm prices, buried the Republican challenger Alf Landon of Kansas, winning 46 of 48 states. It was at the beginning of this campaign, on a wet windy night in Philadelphia, that FDR first used a memorable phrase that would be adopted by a future President Reagan: "To some generations, much is given. Of other generations much is expected. This generation has a rendezvous with history."[12]

During one long cold Iowa winter, Dutch Reagan decided that he would be a much better voice of the Chicago Cubs if he accompanied the team on its spring training trip to Catalina Island, only fifty miles across the water from warm, sun-drenched Los Angeles. Aided by the color and atmosphere he absorbed in spring training, Reagan's broadcasts of the Cubs's games took on new authority, but a strong restlessness gripped him. Sports announcing no longer challenged him—not even the other radio assignments and his own celebrity in the region could stifle the old desire to be an actor. And there was no entangling romance—his hometown sweetheart Margaret Cleaver had returned his ring in 1934, and he had been dating the field ever since.

While in southern California with the Cubs in the spring of 1937, Dutch visited a WHO alumna and friend, Joy Hodges, who was singing with the Jimmy Grier Band at the Biltmore Bowl in Los Angeles. He told her about the Des Moines theater manager who had suggested a screen test and admitted that he had always regarded radio announcing as a path to acting. What did she think—did he have a chance to make it in Hollywood? "Take off your glasses," Joy quickly replied, shaking her head at the heavy black frames. Apprising his good looks and natural manner, she set up an appointment with George Ward of the Meiklejohn Agency who, she promised Dutch, "will be honest with you." But "for Heaven's sake," she said forcefully, "don't see him with those glasses on!"

The very next morning, Ward listened to Dutch outline his acting experience (which he artfully embellished—the Eureka Dramatic Club became the Johnson Professional Players) as well as his salary needs. "Should I go back to Des Moines and forget this," asked the young radio announcer, "or what do I do?" Ward quickly recognized that he could sell the young man before him—with his all-American looks and smile—to the studios.[13]

The agent picked up the telephone and asked for Max Arnow, the casting director at Warner Brothers. "Max," said Ward without any preliminaries, "I have another Robert Taylor in my office." The casting director's booming reply was audible, "God made only one Robert Taylor!" (Ironically, Taylor and Reagan would later become very good friends.) Nevertheless, Arnow invited them over and after sizing up Dutch's broad shoulders and listening to his vibrant voice scheduled a screen test the following Tuesday—a scene from Philip Barry's sophisticated comedy, *Holiday*.

Dutch did the scene, containing some of Barry's most literate dialogue, after the make-up man had tried vainly to do something with his Iowa crew-cut. With the shooting completed at noon, the would-be film actor was informed that it would be several days before the boss Jack Warner could see the film, and he was asked to stand by. To which the young Midwesterner replied, "No, I will be on the train tomorrow—me and the Cubs are going home." On the train, Dutch wondered whether he "had blown the whole thing" but reflected that at least he had a good story to tell his WHO pals.[14] He had done the one thing guaranteed to incite the studio's interest. "Hollywood just *loves* people," he later wrote, "who don't need Hollywood."[15]

One day after he arrived back in Des Moines, a telegram arrived: "Warners offers contract seven years, one year's option, starting at $200 a week. What shall I do? George Ward Meiklejohn Agency." Dutch immediately replied, "Sign before they change their minds." A WHO colleague recalled that the twenty-six-year-old Reagan held court for hours, sitting on his desk, "jubilant, excited, euphoric, accepting everyone's congratulations, mesmerizing all of us with the tales of his Hollywood adventure then, and those yet to be."[16] The small-town boy from Illinois was going to Hollywood to be a movie star and who knew what else.

"Where's the Rest of Me?"

Warner Brothers liked Ronald Reagan very much ("Dutch" quickly disappeared). During his first eleven months, he appeared in eight pictures—a heavy schedule for an actor who had never appeared on a legitimate stage or been inside a film studio. Most young contract players waited months before getting a part, but the studio gambled they could make a leading man out of the tall handsome Reagan. He was immediately given the lead in a sixty-one-minute film called *Love Is in the Air*. Typecast, he played Andy McLeod, a crusading small-town radio announcer who uncovers evidence of a local crime syndicate. It was a B picture as were most of the Warner features in which Reagan appeared for the next few years. But the young actor didn't mind: "All I knew was I was starring in my first movie, and that seemed to make a great deal of sense."[17]

The Warner Brothers studio was run by three brothers and dominated by the oldest, Harry, who believed that all Warner films should have a moral message. "The motion picture," he stated, "presents right and wrong as the Bible does. By showing both right and wrong we teach the right." Jack, the only brother in California, was an outspoken political conservative who required that all his employees fill out a detailed questionnaire that included the question: "Are you a member of any organization, society, group or sect owing allegiance to a foreign government or rule?"[18]

Reagan answered "no" and set about learning the craft of film acting, including how to keep his head still in close-ups, to watch for the chalk marks on the floor that marked his position for a scene, to review the "rushes" of the day's filming; and how to make love, which proved surprisingly difficult. "If you really kiss the girl," he recalled, "it shoves her face out of shape." Relying on his photographic memory, Reagan made it his business to know his part as well as that of the other actor in a scene. He was not bothered by the slow pace of filmmaking nor the retakes when other actors flubbed their lines. He filled the long stretches of idle time by reading voraciously and sharing what he read with fellow actors.

On the set, recalled fellow actor Larry Williams, Reagan would sit down next to him and say, "Larry, before I run down for you this Far Eastern concept I'm sort of kicking around in my mind, answer me a background question: What would you say is the current population of Formosa?" "Ronnie, I don't know things like that." "Right. Most Americans don't. No need to apologize." According to Williams, Reagan seemed to have "the dope on just about everything: this quarter's up-or-down figures on GNP growth, V. I. Lenin's grandfather's occupation, all . . . baseball pitchers' ERAs, the optimistic outlook for California's sugar-beet production. . . . One could not help but be impressed."[19] But it didn't take long for Reagan to realize that most film actors did not share his passionate interest in the world outside Hollywood. He began looking for those who did and found them in the Screen Actors Guild (SAG), affiliated with the conservative American Federation of Labor (AFL), which he was invited to join in 1938.

Even before joining the SAG, he talked openly about the financial inequities of a seven-year contract and the low pay of extras. He surprised his agent at option time by examining every clause in his contract. Told that nothing could be done to change the way Hollywood worked, he replied, "Well, a way has to be figured to turn that around."[20] He now felt secure enough financially to rent a ground-floor apartment for his parents in the flats of West Hollywood, near Beverly Hills. Jack's heart condition severely limited what he could do, but Reagan satisfied his wish to be useful by putting him in charge of his fan mail—and getting Warner Brothers to pay him $25 a week for his work.

Picture swiftly followed picture for the rising young actor—*Hollywood Hotel* (with Dick Powell), *Swing Your Lady* (with Humphrey Bogart), *Sergeant Murphy* (originally bought for James Cagney), *Accidents Will Happen* (in which he played the lead), *Cowboy from Brooklyn* (with Dick Powell and Pat O'Brien), *Boy Meets Girl* (with James Cagney and Pat O'Brien), *Girls on Probation* (starring Reagan), and *Going Places* (with Dick Powell). His career was boosted by gossip columnist Louella Parsons, who also hailed from Dixon, Illinois. In 1939, he began starring in a series of adventure films, playing "Brass" Bancroft, a former army air corps lieutenant who makes a living as a commercial pilot until he joins the Secret Service. (In truth, Reagan hated to fly, preferring to take the train, no matter how long the trip.) He became the Errol Flynn of the B's. "I was as brave as Errol," Reagan later wrote, " but in a low-budget fashion."[21] Today, such "B" films make up much of television's prime time evening programming. Like Flynn, the athletic Reagan did many of his own stunts and was encouraged to do so to save time and money.

Hollywood films during the Depression, biographer Dinesh D'Souza wrote, were usually a combination of traditional values and mainstream aspirations. Because Ronald Reagan embodied those values and aspirations, he was able to portray the heroes who had made America—the citizen-crusader, the lonely sheriff, the battle-weary soldier—and win ever larger audiences for his films.[22]

He was given a lead in what turned out to be a successful film and a solid moneymaker—*Brother Rat,* the story of three cadets at Virginia Military Institute. The other stars were Eddie Albert, Wayne Morris, and Jane Wyman, who became Reagan's romantic interest off camera. With the release of *Brother Rat,* Reagan was assured of steady employment if not yet stardom. That came with *Knute Rockne—All American.* Convinced that a film about the renowned Notre Dame football coach would do well at the box office—and eager to play the legendary doomed halfback George Gipp—Reagan asked everyone he knew how to transform an idea into a picture. And then he picked up a copy of *Variety,* the motion picture trade newspaper, to read that Warner Brothers, his studio, was planning to film the life of Knute Rockne, with Pat O'Brien, with whom he often lunched at Warner's, in the starring role.

An anxious Reagan made an appointment to see producer Hal Wallis, who stunned him by saying he could not see the athletic actor as a football type, particularly Gipp who "was the greatest player in the country." Protests by Reagan that he had played football for eight years in high school and college and had even won a football scholarship had no effect on the skeptical Wallis. He abruptly left the producer's office only to return shortly with several photos of his football days at Eureka College. Wallis examined them closely and then asked, "Can I keep these for a while?" "Sure," said Reagan and drove home slowly. He had been in his house only fifteen minutes when the telephone rang, and the casting office told him to report for a test of the George Gipp part the next day.[23]

Reagan got the role which although it occupied only one reel of the picture was "a nearly perfect part from an actor's standpoint [with] . . . a great entrance, an action middle, and a death scene to finish up." The film ended with Rockne revealing to the Notre Dame team, trailing at half-time in a crucial game, that on his death bed, Gipp had said to him: "Someday, when the team's up against it, breaks are beating the boys, ask them to go in there with all they've got [and] win one for the Gipper."[24] Decades later, "Win One for the Gipper" became a popular motto of Reagan's political campaigns.

Knute Rockne was sneak-previewed in Pasadena in the early fall of 1940. The next morning, while he was still in bed, Warner Brothers telephoned Reagan to tell him he had been cast as the second lead in an Errol Flynn film, *Sante Fe Trail.* In the fitting room at the studio, Reagan watched a wardrobe man rush into the room. Without a word, he gathered up the uniforms of the actor who had initially been cast, threw them into the corner, and hung up new ones in their place. "It occurred to me," recalled Reagan, "that it would be just as easy someday to throw my clothes into the corner and hang some other actor's in their place."[25] The incident remained with Reagan, impressing on him the transitory nature of film acting.

But such bleak possibilities passed quickly from Reagan's mind that day. Life was good. He had acquitted himself well in a dramatic part in a popular film. He had graduated from the B pictures to the A's where he often appeared with one of Warner's most popular stars, Errol Flynn. And he had married (on January 26, 1940) the cutest girl on the Warner lot—Jane Wyman. Columnist Louella Parsons hosted their wedding reception. The Wyman-Reagan marriage was presented in most fan magazines as "a fairy-tale affair"—with Ronnie as the easy-going bachelor and Jane as the free-spirited divorcee (she and her much older first husband had separated shortly after their 1937 wedding when she discovered he did not want children) who would find happiness in an old-fashioned American marriage. "I trusted Ronnie," said Wyman, the child of a broken marriage. "For the first time in my life I truly trusted someone."[26]

The couple demonstrated that it was possible to find God in Hollywood, belonging to the Hollywood Beverly Christian Church. Jane taught Sunday school there, and Reagan continued to contribute to the church for decades even after he joined another congregation. Although admitting that he did not attend Sunday services "as regularly as I should," Reagan revealed that "there hasn't been a serious crisis in my life when I haven't prayed, and when prayer hasn't helped me."[27]

In the world of politics, Reagan's favorite president was running for a third term with the young actor's idolized approval. However, his enthusiasm was tested by an articulate Republican businessman named Justin Dart, who was dating a featured player in one of the "Brother Rat" films. Dart wanted Reagan to understand that more than FDR's leadership was at issue in his bid for a third term, including big-city bosses determined to retain their power and New Dealers who did not want to lose their jobs. Reagan and Dart debated politics and issues for hours. A colleague noted that while still an ardent Roosevelt supporter, Reagan was willing to fault the Democratic Party for the "large federal payrolls."[28] Dart became a good friend of Reagan's and in later years was an unofficial adviser to Governor and then President Reagan.

The parts and the pictures got better and better: *The Badman* with Wallace Beery and Lionel Barrymore; *International Squadron* (released in 1941) in which he played a cocky, wise-cracking American who joins the Royal Air Force and learns to admire the British; and *King's Row*, which made Ronald Reagan an acknowledged star. Reagan played Drake McHugh, a happy-go-lucky ladies' man in a small town who had spent most of his inheritance. His crucial scene came when he awakened in his own bed to realize that his two legs had been amputated by a sadistic surgeon following an accident in a railroad yard. His key line was, "Where's the rest of me?" "Perhaps," he later said, "I never did quite as well again in a single shot." Critics praised the film and Reagan's performance in particular, *Commonweal* calling it "splendid."[29]

The question haunted Reagan far beyond the movie set. In his early autobiography, written in 1963 before he decided to run for public office and while he still thought of himself as primarily an actor, Reagan revealed he had long been searching for an answer. "If [someone] is only an actor," he wrote, "he is much like I was in *King's Row*, only half a man—no matter how great his talents." But he had always loved three things—drama, politics, and sports—"and I'm not sure they always came in that order. In all three of them I came out of the monastery of movies into the world."[30]

How unpredictable the world could be was proven on December 7, 1941, when the Japanese attacked Pearl Harbor, and life was never again the same for anyone in the world.

Gathering War Clouds

King's Row had not yet been released when an envelope stamped, "Immediate Action Active Duty," arrived at Reagan's home in the spring of 1942. He was ready for duty although fully aware of how much he would be giving up professionally and financially. A movie exhibitors' poll had just chosen him as one of five new actors likely to emerge as stars. At Warner Brothers, he had surged into second place in fan mail replacing the veteran star James Cagney and behind only Errol Flynn. A Gallup poll ranked him as among the top one hundred movie stars in the country. The studio was considering him for an upcoming film, *Casablanca;* the part was that of the idealistic anti-Nazi leader Laszlow (ultimately played by Paul Henreid).

Throughout 1940 and 1941, Reagan had argued that America had to get involved in the widening conflict. He did not think that joining the war against Germany was "hawkish" but a commitment to "help the underdog and defend the weak."[31] He also felt a patriotic duty to give something back to the nation that had given him so much. Reagan's passionate interest in the war and politics in general deepened his friendship with the politically active Justin Dart, who introduced him to influential Californians like Goodwin Knight (a future Republican governor of California) and banker Charles Cook. Reagan also spent more time socially with actors George Murphy and Dick Powell, both Republicans and active in the Screen Actors Guild.

"It was a riot," said actress June Allyson, married to Dick Powell at the time, "to listen to Ronnie, a staunch Democrat, trying to convert Richard while Richard argued just as hard to turn Ronnie Republican." When Allyson entered into the conversation, Reagan took her questions seriously, answering them "carefully, methodically." Allyson was impressed, recalling that Jane Wyman ironically advised her, "Don't ask Ronnie what time it is because he will tell you how a watch is made."[32] Wyman's wisecrack was said fondly—the couple were happy and in love. Their first child, Maureen, was born on January 4, 1941, prompting the Hollywood press to describe the Reagans as the perfect family. They began building an eight-room house on a steep hill above Sunset Boulevard in a style the couple called "comfortable Reagan."[33]

Along with his father and fellow Democrats such as Pat O'Brien, Ronald Reagan had celebrated the 1940 reelection of President Roosevelt, who more and more openly expressed concern about the course of the war in Europe. As fervid isolationists and interventionists in and out of Congress squared off, a December 1940 Gallup poll reported that 60 percent of the American people favored helping England, "even at the risk of getting into war ourselves." In February 1941, Wendell Willkie (who had campaigned against Roosevelt for the presidency the previous year) testified for lend-lease before a Congressional committee, assuring its passage.

Reagan's satisfaction about his blooming career and his pride in Roosevelt's leadership were clouded over by the passing of his father. On May 18, 1941, Jack Reagan—shoe salesman, casual Catholic, teller of tall tales, recovering alcoholic—died at the age of fifty-eight. "I'm sure he knows," his son wrote, "that Pat and his new friends were there in the little church off Sunset Boulevard to say goodbye."[34] Reagan later admitted to Edmund Morris that he felt "greater despair [at the funeral] than ever before in his life." But drawing on his faith, he turned to his mother, and said, "I'm okay. Jack is okay and where he is he's very happy."[35]

Reagan found relief in the politics of his profession. When Wyman, a longtime member of the Screen Actors Guild, was asked in July 1941 to become an alternate member of the board, she suggested her husband. "I think he'll make a better alternate than me," she said, adding with a smile, "he might even become president of SAG one day—or maybe America." The board, which included friends like Dick Powell and James Cagney, accepted Reagan, who took his duties seriously. According to biographer Anne Edwards, friends noticed "a change" in Reagan from the time he joined the SAG board—studio and union problems began to share equal time with world conditions in his conversations.[36]

Square Peg in a Square Hole

When he took his preinduction physical examination in early 1942, the doctors demanded to know how Reagan had passed the military's eye test years before. "If we sent you overseas," one exclaimed, "you'd shoot a general." "Yes," replied another, "and you'd miss him." Reagan confessed that he had tricked the examining officer. Otherwise in superb health, he was inducted as a second lieutenant in the U.S. Army, but his papers were stamped, "No combat duty."[37]

His first assignment was Fort Mason, San Francisco, as a liaison officer loading convoys. After a few months, he was transferred from the Army to the Army Air Corps and from Fort Mason to a special "base" outside Los Angeles. The Air Corps was starting a motion picture unit and needed men experienced in filmmaking. Reagan's commanding officer at Fort Mason quickly overrode his young subordinate's doubts: "Whether you're willing or not, you're going—because in thirty-four years, this is the first time I've ever seen the Army make sense. This is putting a square peg in a square hole." And so the square lieutenant returned somewhat self-consciously to Hollywood and his former profession.

Located at the Hal Roach Studios, the Air Corp's motion picture unit was an unusual military installation with 1,300 men and officers and about $200 million worth of film talent—those who served at Fort Roach during the war included Clark Gable, Alan Ladd, Van Johnson, Burgess Meredith, and Arthur Kennedy. It produced dozens of training films and documentaries and conducted a training school for combat camera crews. After an initial assignment as a personnel officer, Reagan became base adjutant or administrative officer and acquired valuable knowledge about bureaucratic decision-making. He also made several films, including *The Rear Gunner,* in which he was the narrator; *For God and Country*; and Irving Berlin's *This Is the Army,* in which he played the army son of George Murphy. (No actor received any studio pay for his work in *This Is the Army*, and Warner's turned over the profits to Army Relief.) Between takes, Murphy and Reagan found time for "animated debate" about politics with the older Murphy urging the younger actor to take a more conservative viewpoint.

Passionate in his patriotism, Reagan was a regular at bond drives and troop send-offs. While juggling administrative and theatrical duties at Fort Roach, Reagan was promoted to captain and then to major which he asked to be cancelled, asking, "Who was I to be a major for serving in California without ever hearing a shot fired in anger?"[38]

In January 1944, Reagan was featured in a one-hour national radio broadcast to sell war bonds, playing a soldier in a foxhole on the front lines. Among the others who appeared in the broadcast were Treasury Secretary Henry J. Morgenthau Jr., General Dwight D. Eisenhower, and Bing Crosby. The usually acerbic Morgenthau subsequently wrote Reagan that "this was the most effective program of its kind since the beginning of the war."[39]

But Fort Roach was not just in the entertainment business, working, for example, on two important classified projects. The first concerned the destruction of the Nazi V-2 rocket launching sites at Peenemunde, Germany. The rockets were damaging buildings and civilian morale in England and would have affected the Normandy invasion if they had continued to operate at full efficiency. Exact replicas of the sites were built in Florida and experimental bombings were carried out to discover how best to destroy the rocket installations. Camera crews at Fort Roach filmed the raids. The films were flown to the Eighth Air Force in England, which knocked out enough sites, Reagan reported, "to postpone the V-2 launchings long enough for D-Day to take place on schedule."[40]

An even more secret project dealt with the war in the Pacific. As American airplanes drew closer and closer to the heart of Japan, film experts at Fort Roach concluded that bomber crews could reduce their losses and improve their efficiency if they had more precise information about their targets. The special effects crew built a complete miniature of Tokyo that filled a sound stage. They erected a crane and camera mount above the model city and photographed it, creating the on-screen effect of movies taken from an airplane flying at various heights and speeds.

A group of generals were invited to the studio and shown movies of Tokyo taken by real airplanes flying over the city along with movies of the model Tokyo. Challenged to identify which was which, they failed. "Skepticism [about the project] turned to enthusiasm," wrote Reagan, and the sound stage was put under twenty-four-hour guard and admission was limited to authorized personnel.[41] Additional models of other Japanese cities were constructed, and the special effects men became so proficient they could show a bomb run as seen through the bombsight and even portray what the target would look like in darkness and bad weather. Reagan was the narrator of the bombing runs and described the entire flight from the first sighting of the target to the command, "Bombs away!"

To maintain authenticity, film of actual raids would be immediately flown to Los Angeles so that "we could burn out portions of our target scene and put in the scars of the bombing." Through such scrupulous editing, "our film would always look exactly the way the target would appear to the crews going in on the next run." Here, said Reagan with satisfaction, "was the true magic of motion picture making."[42]

As the war drew to a close, Captain Reagan had his first direct encounter with civilian bureaucracy, resulting, he wrote, in "the first crack in my staunch liberalism." As we have seen, his liberalism had already been seriously tested through countless debates with conservative colleagues in radio and films, ranging from H. R. Gross at WHO Des Moines to Dick Powell at Warner Brothers as well as Justin Dart. Civil Service now informed base adjutant Reagan that 250 civilians would shortly be arriving at Fort Roach, accompanied by their records that "filled shelves from floor to ceiling, around virtually four walls of a barrack-sized building." Unfortunately, not all the civilians could fill their jobs.[43]

An officer-writer came storming into Reagan's office, declaring he had to have a new secretary—one who could at least spell "cat"! The civilian personnel director had responded that all the complaining officer had to do was to sign formal charges and testify—in a public hearing—to his secretary's incompetence. Repelled by such a procedure, the officer refused to sign a complaint. Reagan wondered if there wasn't some other way of solving the officer's problem. As he suspected, his civilian counterpart had a ready bureaucratic answer: she would transfer a qualified secretary to the unhappy officer and move the girl who couldn't spell *cat* to another officer at a higher salary, thereby pleasing everyone and upsetting no one.

"No one in the administrative hierarchy of Civil Service," Reagan wrote, "will ever interfere with this upgrading process because his own pay and rating are based on the number of employees beneath him and the grades of those employees. It's a built-in process for empire building."[44] As governor and president, Ronald Reagan devoted much of his time to disassembling such empires.

CHAPTER 3

Communism and Capitalism

S ERIOUS STRIKES HAD BEGUN IN HOLLYWOOD even before the war's end as unions fought for jurisdiction of a $5 billion a year industry whose films were seen by 500 million Americans every week. Between 1945 and 1947, there were half a dozen major strikes in the film capital, costing moviemakers approximately $150 million in production costs. About eight thousand workers lost an estimated 9 million man hours and some $28 million in wages. The costly struggle was caused in part by Communist attempts to seize control of one of the most important media in America.

The Communists's role was not obvious or even admitted by many in Hollywood, including Ronald Reagan, who was at the time admittedly naive about communism, influenced by America's wartime alliance with the Soviet Union. "I thought," he said, "the nearest Communists were fighting in Stalingrad." He described himself as a "near hopeless hemophilic liberal." Following his discharge from the Army Air Corps at the end of 1945, he joined every organization "that would guarantee to save the world,"[1] among them the United World Federalists and later Americans for Democratic Action.

For a year, Reagan made speeches denouncing fascism to enthusiastic applause. Then one night, at the suggestion of a minister friend, he added a new last paragraph also denouncing communism. The audience sat sullen and silent, forcing Reagan to realize that the people he had been talking to were curiously one-sided in their views. He cut back on his speaking, especially for the ultra-Left American Veterans Committee, and began intensely researching current politics. He came to recognize the signs of Communist activity in the film industry and the importance of the Screen Actors Guild (SAG), of which he was a director, in trying to settle the still continuing jurisdictional strike.

SAG's efforts became all-important as violence increased. Autos were overturned. Clubs, chains, bottles, bricks, and two-by-four planks were used in scuffles between the warring unions. Homes of members were bombed and individuals were mugged. SAG volunteered as a mediator and came close to finding a solution on several occasions, but each time its efforts failed, often at the very last moment. The reason why was later revealed by state investigators. "The Communist Party working in Hollywood," reported a committee of the California Legislature, "wanted control over everything that moved on wheels. . . . They soon moved Communist units into those unions having jurisdiction over carpenters, painters, musicians, grips and electricians. To control these trade unions was to control the motion picture industry."[2]

The strike, which was finally settled when responsible union leaders endorsed the position of the old-line International Alliance of Theatrical State Employees, had a profound impact on Ronald Reagan. "I owe it to that period," he wrote, "that I managed to sort out a lot of items in my personal life. From being an active (although unconscious) partisan in what now and then turned out to be communist causes, I little by little became . . . awakened."[3]

One man who helped awaken him was George Murphy, a former SAG president and later U.S. senator from California, who explained to me that he had paid more attention to the activities and programs of the Communists than other SAG members. When he tried to explain what was going on "to Ron . . . he thought I was trying to convince him he ought to be a Republican." When Reagan discovered the truth about the Communists, according to Murphy, he "swung around hard and became an active Republican—just as I did."[4]

That Ronald Reagan evolved into a committed anticommunist was confirmed by actor Sterling Hayden in testimony before the House Committee on Un-American Activities. Hayden revealed that he had been for a short time a member of the Communist Party. Describing the Party's efforts to persuade film actors and actresses to support a communist-led strike in Hollywood, Hayden was asked what stopped them. He replied that they "ran into the board of directors of the SAG and particularly into Ronnie Reagan, who was a one-man battalion."[5]

As a result of his anticommunist offensive (which included giving information to the Federal Bureau of Investigation about such ultra-Left groups as the American Veterans Committee and the Hollywood Independent Citizens Committee of Arts, Sciences and Professions—HICCASP), Reagan began receiving threats against his life. One night, on location, he was called to a telephone and heard an unidentified voice say, "There's a group being formed to deal with you. They're going to fix you so you won't ever act again."[6] The next day, at the insistence of friends and associates, Warner Brothers arranged for the police to issue Reagan a license to carry a gun: he wore a loaded .32-caliber Smith & Wesson revolver in a shoulder holster for months. Reagan learned firsthand how the other side would try to twist and turn the truth to its advantage: at one HICCASP board meeting, one pro-communist recited the Soviet Constitution to prove that "Russia was more democratic than the United States."[7]

During this turbulent period, Reagan was elected president of the 15,000-member SAG, succeeding Robert Montgomery. In all, he was elected president six times—more than any other actor in Hollywood until that time, primarily for his widely acknowledged negotiating skill. He also served on SAG's board of directors for sixteen years and received several awards for his union activities, including a certificate from the American Newspaper Guild (CIO) for "spearheading the fight against communism in Hollywood" and from the AFL Auto Workers Union.[8] He would later point out proudly that he was the first union leader to be elected president.

In summing up the long months of struggle against the Communists, Reagan wrote that "we fought on the issues and proved that if you keep the people informed on those issues, they won't make a mistake." In an interview with columnist Hedda Hopper in May 1947, he articulated a fundamental principle to which he would adhere as governor and president: "Our highest aim should be the cultivation of freedom of the individual, for therein lies the highest dignity of man. Tyranny is tyranny and—whether it comes from the Right, Left or Center—it is evil." The way to fight communism, he said, was to improve America.[9]

His duties as SAG president were many and demanding. He was called to Washington in October 1947 to testify before the House Committee on Un-American Activities about Communist infiltration of Hollywood. He stated that while he abhorred the "fifth column" tactics of the Communists, he would not want to see "our country . . . compromise with any of our democratic principles" through fear of communism or any other ideology.[10] Reagan and two former SAG presidents—George Murphy and Robert

Montgomery—won praise from *Life*, the *New York Times*, and other major publications for their testimony, rooted in a firm anticommunism and a no less firm faith in liberal democracy. A decade later, Reagan exercised one of those democratic principles—the right to dissent—by refusing, as SAG president, to attend a party given by 20th Century Fox for visiting Soviet Premier Nikita Khrushchev, responsible for the brutal Soviet suppression of the Hungarian Revolution in 1956.

While publicly stating that he opposed the creation of any "blacklist" of people who should not be employed for political reasons, Reagan acknowledged the right of film studios to take into consideration actors' outside activities when employing them. As he put it in a letter to *Playboy* publisher Hugh Hefner more than a decade later, "Hollywood has no blacklist. Hollywood does have a list handed to it by millions of 'moviegoers' who have said 'we don't want and will not pay to see pictures made by or with these people we consider traitors.'"[11] "Traitor" is a strong word, but in the opinion of millions of Americans in the late 1940s and into the 1950s, it was an appropriate word for people who sided with the Soviet Union in the Cold War.

Reagan later conceded that his long association with the Screen Actors Guild and the serious side of Hollywood hurt his movie career but expressed little regret, saying, "Would I do it again? Yes . . . [because] I think you have to do something to pay your way in life." Vice president Taft Schreiber of Music Corporation of America (MCA)—which represented Reagan starting in the late thirties—corroborated Reagan's deep commitment to public service, stating, "It was rare that anyone as young and as involved in screen work would give of himself to the extent required, for it meant . . . giving many extracurricular hours . . . that only the most dedicated would choose to undertake."[12]

Reagan's ever-present SAG responsibilities and his intense interest in national politics also took their toll on his marriage. On June 29, 1948, after months of attempted reconciliation, Jane Wyman filed suit and was granted a divorce on grounds of mental cruelty. "In recent months," she told the judge, "my husband and I engaged in continual arguments on his political views . . . finally there was nothing in common between us . . . nothing to sustain our marriage."[13] Wyman found a house in Malibu for herself and the two children, Maureen and Michael, whom the Reagans adopted in March 1945. The father was free to visit them and frequently did so. "If only I hadn't been so busy," Reagan later conceded, he might have seen the warning signs. The year leading up to the divorce had been especially difficult for both Reagans. On June 26, 1947, Jane gave birth to a baby girl who was four months premature and died the same day. Ronnie was not there because he was fighting for his life with viral pneumonia at another hospital; it took four months for him to recover. Again a bachelor, Reagan eschewed night clubs and dated sporadically, preferring to spend his time at the SAG offices, seeking good films, and seeing his children and his mother Nelle.[14]

For Reagan, the most important dividend of his union presidency was a 1949 meeting with an aspiring young actress named Nancy Davis, who had large dark-brown eyes and a delicate beauty. Director Mervyn LeRoy asked the SAG president to help the young woman whose name kept appearing—without her approval—on Communist front rosters. After confirming that Davis was a vocal anticommunist (and the daughter of a well-known Chicago neurosurgeon), Reagan decided to reassure the young actress in person over an early dinner at Chasen's, a favorite restaurant of Reagan's. The couple found they had so much to share that the evening did not end until 3:30 A.M.

Born in 1921, Nancy was a graduate of Girls Latin School in Chicago and Smith College who came by her interest in acting familially—her mother Edith Luckett had toured with the famed George M. Cohan and later appeared in dozens of plays on and off Broadway with such actors as Zasu Pitts, Spring Byington, Pat O'Brien, and Spencer Tracy. Her adopted father was Dr. Loyal Davis, a widely respected physician and large contributor to the Republican Party. Davis had married Edith in 1929 and formally adopted Nancy in 1935. A close bond immediately developed between the somewhat stern man of medicine and the pretty little girl who called her new father "Dad" from the first day.[15] Loyal Davis's conservative politics became the politics of the daughter who wanted to please her new father. And they provided an essential bond between Nancy Davis and Ronald Reagan.

"Ronnie made me aware of all that was going on," Nancy told me. "That was one of the first things that impressed me and attracted me to him. He had so many other interests beside the film business—I can't remember him talking about his last picture."[16] Ronnie and Nancy dated for nearly two years before they decided to get married on March 4, 1952, at the Little

Brown Church in the Valley in North Hollywood, with William Holden as best man and Mrs. Holden as matron of honor. Nancy happily stopped acting after a modest career of eight films (including *Hellcats of the Navy* with Ronald Reagan), explaining, "If you try to make two careers work, one of them has to suffer. Maybe some women can do it, but not me."[17] They would have two children—Patricia Ann (Patti), born in late 1952, and Ronald Prescott (Skipper), born in 1958.

Despite the Hollywood attempt to present her as the model of a 1950s wife, Nancy Reagan was never, as Lou Cannon points out, "the little woman" in the kitchen. She was socially sophisticated, politically aware, and had what she called a better "antenna" about her husband's associates than he did—and did not hesitate to express her opinion about them. Particularly after his entry into politics, those who dealt with Ronald Reagan discovered that things went much smoother if they had Nancy's approval.[18] They became so close with the passing of the years that nothing—not even their children—could come between them. "Sometimes," Reagan later wrote, "I think my life really began when I met Nancy."[19]

Looking for a Good Part

A good picture is hard to find, especially for a politically active actor like Ronald Reagan better known for what he did off screen than on. Also, the public no longer depended exclusively on movies for its entertainment—television was casting its flickering shadow across the nation and Hollywood. And the public—especially those under twenty—was no longer, in Reagan's words, "oohing and aahing over Robert Taylor, Jimmy Stewart, or Tyrone Power, let alone me." Young Americans had come to ticket-buying while the older stars were off-screen during World War II—and "they had a new set of heroes."[20]

In 1946, super-agent Lew Wasserman of MCA had negotiated an impressive million-dollar contract for Ronald Reagan—Warner Brothers agreed to pay him $3,500 a week for seven years with nine weeks' layoff each year—which translated into a minimum of $150,000 a year. It was a princely sum for an actor that Warner's clearly considered a star. In 1946, Reagan earned just under $170,000, almost as much as Errol Flynn. In the late forties and early fifties, Reagan starred in good films such as *The Hasty Heart* with Patricia Neal and *The Winning Team* with Doris Day, clunkers such as *That Hagen Girl* with Shirley Temple and *Night unto Night* with Viveca Lindfors, and moneymakers like *Bedtime for Bonzo* with Bonzo the chimpanzee and *The Last Outpost* with Rhonda Fleming. At forty and no longer able to play the brash young all-American, Reagan noted that his box office appeal was slowly declining. The resourceful Wasserman negotiated a new contract with Warner that gave Reagan the right to do outside pictures—he was now a freelance actor.

Independence, he discovered, did not assure affluence. With the new baby Patti and bills beginning to accumulate, Reagan had the choice of either taking whatever offer came along or waiting for the right part in the right picture. For fourteen months, during most of 1952 and 1953, he—with Nancy's approval—turned down nearly every script offered him, one exception being *Prisoner of War,* a film about the brainwashing of American POWs in North Korea. Unfortunately, the film was hurriedly produced and did not do as well at the box office as Reagan hoped it would. Reagan placed television on the "won't do" list because he believed that an actor who did a TV series would be forever identified with the role.

When his agent suggested a nightclub act, Reagan reluctantly agreed, assured that his part was that of an emcee and not a baggy-pants comic. The act sold out for two weeks in February 1954 at the Last Frontier casino in Las Vegas—with Reagan humorously commenting about his film acting days and working with one act in a comedy routine—and elicited offers from the Waldorf in New York and top clubs in Chicago and Miami. Reagan's easy way with a quip may have been, in part, genetic, but was more likely due to his frequent lunches at Chasen's in the late forties and early fifties with the writers for Bob Hope, Jack Benny, and other leading comedians of the day. He was allowed to join the professional joke writers, who were always looking for new material, on one condition—that he bring a new joke with him each time. Reagan readily agreed, he later explained, in order to improve the humorous content of his public speeches.[21] It was another example of Reagan's thorough, disciplined approach to whatever he attempted. But he was not tempted by the life of an itinerant entertainer, however well-paid, and he and Nancy went home to ride and raise horses and cattle on their 370-acre ranch, Yearling Row, in the Malibu Hills.

Reagan had plenty of time to consider the future: in August 1952, he had resigned as president of the Screen Actors Guild after serving longer than any other person during its nineteen years. According to SAG director John Dales, Reagan stepped down because he feared that he was becoming too powerful a chief executive, once remarking to Dales, "Jack . . . is there anything I can't get out of the board?" However, he remained a SAG director and continued to expound his outspoken anticommunist beliefs.[22]

Those beliefs led him to an increasing involvement in national politics, although he rejected all invitations to run for public office. In mid-1946, he was approached by Democrats to run for Congress, but declined, explaining, "I couldn't go around making speeches without feeling I was doing it for self-glorification." In 1948, he vigorously campaigned for President Harry S Truman and other Democrats, introducing the incumbent president at an evening rally at Gilmore Field in Los Angeles. He cut a number of radio spots for major Democratic political candidates and causes, including one for the International Ladies Garment Workers Union, in which he said that "the Republican 80th Congress and the National Association of Manufacturers . . . [brought] on inflation and set back the cause of liberal government in the United States."[23]

In 1950, he backed ultraliberal Helen Gahagan Douglas, who was defeated by Congressman Richard M. Nixon in a calumny-laden U.S. Senate race in California.[24] When I asked Reagan about the extent of his commitment to Douglas (described by Nixon and other Republicans as the "Pink Lady"), he chose his words carefully, "As a Democrat, I supported the ticket from top to bottom."[25] He could not have been enthusiastic because their views about communism were far apart. "I believe," he wrote at the time in a guest column for labor columnist Victor Riesel, "that all participants in the international Communist conspiracy against our nation should be exposed for what they are—enemies of our country and of our form of government."[26]

Reagan paid for his political bluntness "There is no question," he told biographer Lou Cannon that "my career suffered from anticommunism." Interviewing Reagan in 1980, a reporter was struck by the "cold fury" the presidential candidate displayed when recalling his encounters with film colony Communists. "I discovered it firsthand," Reagan said, "the cynicism, the brutality, the complete lack of morality in their positions, and the cold-bloodedness of their attempt, at any cost, to gain control of that industry." President Reagan's willingness to call a Communist a Communist can be traced to his personal experience with Hollywood Communists in the 1940s.[27]

It was in the summer of 1952 that Reagan first publicly described America as divinely led. He was the commencement speaker at William

Woods College, a small women's college in Fulton, Missouri, where Winston Churchill had delivered his famous "Iron Curtain" speech six years earlier. Reagan said, "I believe that God in shedding his grace on this country has always in this divine scheme of things kept an eye on our land and guided it as a promised land." As biographer Paul Kengor points out, you can draw a straight line from these 1952 words to his 1983 address to religious broadcasters during his presidency when he remarked: "I've always believed that this blessed land was set apart in a special way, that some divine plan placed this great continent here between the two oceans to be found by people from every corner of the Earth—people who had a special love for freedom."[28]

In 1952, although still registered as a Democrat, Ronald Reagan voted for Republican Dwight D. Eisenhower while expressing prescient reservations about his running mate to an old friend: "Nixon . . . is *less than honest* and . . . completely undeserving of the high honor paid him."[29] He inched closer to active politics in 1953 when he headed Los Angeles Mayor Fletcher Bowron's reelection campaign, but in an advisory capacity. Subsequently, he was approached by conservative Republican Holmes Tuttle about running for the U.S. Senate but turned down the offer "with thanks."[30] Like Justin Dart, Holmes Tuttle would become an adviser and then a member of Reagan's Kitchen Cabinet.

And then came the opportunity that gave Reagan a new career and completed his political transformation from liberal Democrat to conservative Republican.

Rendezvous with Destiny

General Electric was looking for a new television program that would last. Revue Productions, a subsidiary of MCA, believed it had the answer—a weekly half-hour dramatic series featuring top Hollywood stars with Ronald Reagan as the host and occasional lead. What made the proposal particularly appealing to General Electric was that Reagan agreed to make personal appearances at all of GE's plants as part of the company's Employee and Community Relations Program. And so in the fall of 1954, *GE Theater* began an eight-year run, emanating from both New York and Hollywood and alternating between live and filmed programs. For seven of the eight years, it was ranked first in a prime viewing slot—nine o'clock Sunday night.

GE Theater made Reagan a star in what was becoming the most important entertainment medium in the nation. It brought him financial security with an annual salary of $125,000 that reached $165,000 annually when he became part owner of the series. And it put him on the road from coast to coast talking to people in thirty-one different states (soon, he was speaking to civic, fraternal, and other groups in the cities where GE plants were located). "He was tall, trim, dashing," and had the added advantage of "being a movie star without acting like one."[31] Reagan has estimated that he visited all 135 of General Electric's plants and personally met with most of its 250,000 plant employees. He got to know the likes and dislikes of these everyday citizens, remarking that too many political leaders "have underestimated them."[32] A presidential candidate could not have asked for any better training than Ronald Reagan's eight-year odyssey across America as GE's spokesman, traveling to every corner of the country, speaking to every variety of American, talking about and answering questions about the primary issues of the day.

The community relations part of his job started more slowly, but in a few months he was talking to dozens of civic and educational organizations about Hollywood—especially the attempted takeover of the film capital by the Communists. He was disturbed to discover how uninformed the average audience was about communism and how it operated. He determined to educate them, and in the process his speeches began to mention collectivism along with communism. "The Hollywood portion of the talk shortened and disappeared," he admitted. "The warning words of what could happen changed to concrete examples of what has already happened, and I learned very early to document those examples."[33]

The initial GE tour in August 1954 began at the giant plant in Schenectady, New York. Earl B. Dunckel, a former newspaperman assigned by the company to accompany Reagan, recalled that as soon as the movie actor stepped on to the factory floor workers recognized him and the machines stopped. Reagan walked the plant's thirty-one cement acres for four hours stopping at each machine, talking to nearly every employee. "The women came running up," remembered Dunckel, with mash notes and autographs while the men stood back, "obviously saying something derogatory like 'I bet he's a fag.'" Then Reagan walked over to the men and engaged them in conversation, telling a joke or two. When he left them ten minutes later, "they were all slapping him on the back saying, 'That's the way, Ron.'"[34] It was a demonstration of Reagan's "almost mystical ability to achieve an empathy with almost any audience."[35]

While still in Schenectady, Reagan was asked to address a convention of several thousand high school teachers when their speaker fell ill. When Dunckel pointed out that Reagan already had a full schedule and would have almost no time to prepare his remarks, a quietly confident Reagan said, "Dunk, let's give it a try." When Reagan finished talking about education the next evening, Dunckel remembered, "he got a good ten-minute standing applause," and the public affairs representative realized "the breadth and depth of his knowledge . . . everything that went into that mind stayed there."[36]

And however busy Reagan was, he did not turn aside anyone who approached him, especially a young person seeking advice. One night when Reagan and his GE companion came back to their Erie, Pennsylvania, hotel, dog-tired after a long day, they were greeted by a stage-struck small-town girl who had been sitting in the lobby for four hours. She wanted to be an actress, she explained eagerly—what should she do? Reagan did not brush her off but patiently sat and talked with the young woman in the lobby for an hour and a half. "Do things right there in Erie, Pennsylvania," he advised her. "Get on radio, get on television, get in the little theater." If she could win an audience in Erie, he assured her, she could win an audience anywhere.[37] Despite the Hollywood aura that unquestionably surrounded him, he seemed to be without vanity. Dunckel said that when they arrived at the usual two-bedroom hotel suite, he and Reagan would flip a coin, with the winner getting the big room and the loser the small one.

George Dalen, a former FBI agent, succeeded Dunckel and accompanied Reagan around the country, north, south, east, and west, for the ensuing six years. They always traveled by train because Reagan had a fear of flying, traceable to a bad flight to Catalina in 1937. He did not fly again for thirty years until campaigning for governor of California obliged him to accept that he had no alternative. Dalen confirmed the film actor's lack of pretense, recounting the time they were on a night train from Providence, Rhode Island, to New York City, that was stalled by a snow storm. There was no food service but Reagan had a box of jellybeans ("which he regularly carried") and the porter had a thermos of coffee. Sitting in the porter's quarters, the three men shared the jellybeans, coffee and a couple of bags of popcorn all the way into New York. "It was not a question of making a gesture," Dalen said, "it was just the natural and human thing to do so he did it."[38]

On a typical day, Reagan would breakfast with the local press, meet GE employees including shop workers, secretaries, managers, and engineers, talk to city officials, visit GE distributors and dealers, speak to clubs such as the Chamber of Commerce and Rotary, and address students at local schools. He attracted people's attention because he was a Hollywood star, but he retained their attention because he was "so articulate and well-informed."[39] He always wore a shirt and tie; his dark hair was carefully combed and his shoes were highly polished. He projected an air of calm and maturity, aware of his position as a spokesman for a leading American corporation and, increasingly, for American conservatism. "Of course he inherited an Irish temper," his secretary Helene von Damm later commented. But when she caught him using four-letter words, he would "blush and utter an embarrassed apology."[40]

Sometimes he ran into opposition. He was scheduled to speak at a Los Angeles convention in 1959 when George Dalen informed him that a federal government official had strongly protested to GE about Reagan's proposed speech, specifically his using the Tennessee Valley Authority (TVA) as an example of how government programs can expand beyond their original purpose. There had been pointed references to the millions of dollars of business that General Electric did with the government that might be placed in jeopardy. Reagan asked how GE president Ralph Cordiner (whom he knew personally and who often gave him a book "you ought to read") had reacted and was told that he had informed the federal bureaucrat that GE "would not tell any individual what he could not say."

However, concerned that his speech might affect GE's government contracts and the jobs of GE employees, Reagan called Cordiner in New York. "It's my problem, and I've taken it on," said the GE executive, expressing regret that Reagan had learned about the protest and implied threat. Impressed by Cordiner's willingness to stand up for him, Reagan decided to reciprocate. "Mr. Cordiner," he asked, "what would you say if I said I could make my speech just as effectively without mentioning TVA?" After a pause, the reply came, "Well, it would make my job easier." Dropping TVA from his speech was no real sacrifice, Reagan later wrote, because "you can reach out blindfolded and grab a hundred examples of overgrown government." But, he added, the governmental effort to censor his remarks—and in the middle of a Republican administration—illustrated "how late it is if we are to save freedom."[41] The incident inspired Reagan to become even more politically aware and active.

That same year, the Screen Actors Guild elevated him once again to the presidency because it wanted the best possible negotiator in a bitter battle with the film studios over the issue of television residual pay for actors. There was a five-week strike—the first in the guild's history—and when Reagan presented the strike-settlement package to a mass meeting of the SAG membership in April 1960, he received a standing ovation and a landslide approval vote of 6,399 to 259.[42]

Cordiner, one of the nation's most respected businessmen, expressed to me his admiration for Reagan's ability to communicate with any audience large or small. "I think," he said, that people were impressed "with his sincerity, his thoughtfulness and his forthrightness." He was always struck by Reagan's habit, unusual "for so busy a man," of "personally studying a subject." Cordiner called Reagan "a student" who "does not appear before an audience, write a speech, deliver a paper or even have a discussion with a very small group unless he has researched and reviewed the subject." He emphasized that Ronald Reagan had been a "unanimous" choice as host of the *GE Theater* and a spokesman for GE because he could articulate the "important issues and some of the basic truths" that were "being forgotten or ignored."[43]

Both Dunckel and Dalen confirmed Reagan's studious ways, describing how he would read newspapers, magazines (*Reader's Digest* was a favorite) and books for hours on the long train rides between GE plants and cities, underlining passages and making notes for his talks. As they traveled, Dunckel in particular would talk conservative politics. As he had with H. R. Gross, Justin Dart, Dick Powell, and George Murphy, Reagan at first attempted to defend the New Deal but at last agreed (in a formulation he would use as a candidate) that the Democratic Party "had turned the corner and gone a different direction. He had not deserted it—it had deserted him."[44] But as with so many Americans who lived through the Depression and then World War II, Reagan never deserted FDR, always crediting his exemplary leadership during some of the most testing times in American history.

For seven years, Sunday night at nine belonged to General Electric's thirty-minute dramatic series, featuring such stars as Bob Hope, Jack

Benny, Ethel Barrymore, and James Dean. Reagan himself starred in thirty-five of the programs along with a wide range of female stars including Kim Hunter, Cloris Leachman, Geraldine Page, Agnes Moorehead, Peggy Lee, Anne Baxter, Jeanne Crain, and his wife Nancy. But the GE *Theater* met its match in the eighth year—an hour-long technicolor Western called *Bonanza*. As ratings fell, GE talked with CBS and its advertising agency about its options, including a new format, but Reagan responded he was not interested. Another factor in GE's decision to cancel the show and to let their host go was that Reagan was no longer just a Hollywood and television actor. His politics were now very visible and openly Republican, although the philosophical content of what he said had changed very little since the mid-1950s.

Big Government and its debilitating effects on life and liberty had been his central theme during the Eisenhower years and had been generally accepted as nonpartisan. Titles of his talks included "Tax Curbs" and "Business, Ballots and Bureaus" (about the evils of burgeoning government). "If I had to choose one word to describe the salient characteristic of the revolution of our times," he would say, "the word would be *collectivism*—the tendency to center the power of all initiative in one central government." But the same analysis after the inaugural of President Kennedy in January 1961 "brought down thunders of wrath on my head, the charge that my speech was a partisan political attack, an expression of right wing extremism." Reluctantly, Reagan conceded that many so-called liberals were not liberal— "they will defend to the death [only] your right to agree with them."[45]

In the 1960 presidential contest, and still a Democrat, he worked hard for Richard Nixon, making by his estimate some two hundred speeches across the country. "I literally traveled the same kind of campaign route the candidate himself traveled," said Reagan, who did not find the pace particularly onerous. Although he had been privately critical of Nixon in 1952, he now publicly and enthusiastically supported him, in large part because of the politics of his opponent John F. Kennedy, whom he considered a socialist. "Under the tousled boyish haircut," he wrote Nixon in 1960, "it is still old Karl Marx. . . . There is nothing new in the idea of a government being Big Brother to us all."[46]

Unwilling to be "a professional Democrat for Republican candidates," Reagan registered in 1962 as a Republican and supported Nixon's unsuccessful bid against Governor Edmund (Pat) Brown, whom, ironically,

Reagan would challenge just four years later.[47] That same year, he served as honorary campaign chairman for Loyd Wright, a prominent conservative and lawyer, in the Republican primary against incumbent senator Thomas Kuchel, an equally prominent liberal. His accelerating political involvement was overcast by the death of his mother Nelle on July 25, 1962, at the age of seventy-nine. Nelle Reagan spent the last four years of her life in a Santa Monica nursing home suffering from Alzheimer's. It took Reagan several months to recover from her passing, even with Nancy's help.

No longer bound by any affiliation with General Electric (although he was host of the nonnetwork television series, *Death Valley Days,* for much of 1965 and early 1966), Reagan found release in politics. Wherever he went and for whomever he campaigned, Reagan stuck to his conservative principles. Conservatives believed, he said, that "the collective responsibility of qualified men in a community" should decide the course of that community while liberals believed in "remote and massive strong-arming from afar, usually Washington, D.C." Conservatives believed in "the unique powers of the individual" while liberals leaned increasingly toward bureaucracy and "forced fiat."[48] Other conservatives, especially Senator Barry Goldwater of Arizona, were saying the same things, but few equaled Reagan's ability to be both principled and persuasive. The pressure continued to mount for Reagan to campaign for himself rather than others. But in politics, as in most professions, timing is everything, and the timing was not yet right for candidate Ronald Reagan.

"A Time for Choosing"

Goldwater and Reagan had known each other since the early 1950s when Ronald and Nancy had begun visiting her parents in sunny Phoenix, to which they had retired from the icy winds and winters of Chicago. Although never personally close, the two conservatives shared a passionate love of country and freedom and a no less fervent anticommunism. Reagan admired Goldwater's championing of conservatism and willingly campaigned for him in 1964, but he limited himself mostly to appearances in California because he was still the host of *Death Valley Days.* He also agreed to serve as the largely ceremonial cochairman of California Citizens for Goldwater-Miller. In the early fall, several wealthy California Republicans, led by Holmes Tuttle and Henry Salvatori, asked Reagan whether he would repeat the remarks he had been making outlining the case for Goldwater on national television. "Sure," Reagan replied, "if you think it would do any good." The money was raised for a half-hour on NBC, and Reagan filmed his speech, essentially a distillation of the limited government, anticommunist themes he had articulated as a spokesman for GE. But there was a critical difference—this was a speech for a political candidate seeking the presidency, and Reagan emphasized how important the choice between Goldwater and Lyndon B. Johnson was for America and the world.[49]

Two days before the program was to air—on Tuesday, October 27, one week before election day—an uncomfortable Goldwater telephoned a puzzled Reagan. Some of his advisers, said the senator, were worried about references in Reagan's address to social security, an issue that had plagued Goldwater since the New Hampshire primary when he had suggested that the system might benefit from a voluntary option. "Barry," Reagan reassured his fellow conservative, "I've been making the speech all over [California] for quite a while, and I have to tell you, it's been well received, including whatever remarks I've made about Social Security."

"Well," Goldwater said, "I haven't heard or seen the speech yet. They've got a tape here, so I'll run it and call you back." After the senator listened to an audiotape, he asked his advisers, "What the hell's wrong with that?" Reagan's remarks about Social Security were in fact similar to Goldwater's long-held position. Goldwater called Reagan and gave his approval for a thirty-minute televised speech that made political history.[50]

The speech was pure Reagan: it was filled with facts and quips—"a government bureau is the nearest thing to eternal life we'll ever see on this earth!" It took firm stands on controversial issues—"every responsible farmer and farm organization has repeatedly asked the government to free the farm economy, but who are farmers to know what is best for them?" It was dramatic and poetic—"we are at war with the most dangerous enemy that has ever faced mankind in his long climb from the swamp to the stars."[51]

Reagan delivered it superbly (before an audience of mostly young conservatives) because he had written it himself and believed what he had written. It was the product of his own thinking and research over the years. It was the essence of his anticommunist, anticollectivist philosophy which now received its first national exposure. The political scientist Hugh Heclo called Reagan's vision "sacramental" because it interpreted the American experience as "something sacred, a material phenomenon expressing a spiritual reality." According to Heclo, Reagan believed that "God had chosen America as the agent of His special purposes in history"; that America was sanctified as a "rescuing, redeemer nation"; and that America had broken the historic pattern of nations rising, growing, declining, and falling.[52]

And indeed a belief in America's exceptionalism suffused the October 1964 speech. Reagan described America, borrowing from Abraham Lincoln, as "the last best hope of man on earth" and then quoted Winston Churchill that "there is something going on in time and space, and beyond time and space, which, whether we like it or not, spells duty." America had come, Reagan said bluntly, to "a time for choosing" between free enterprise and big government—between individual liberty and "the ant heap of totalitarianism." He challenged his viewers: "Are you willing to spend time studying the issues, making yourself aware, and then conveying that information to family and friends?" Borrowing language from his favorite president, Franklin D. Roosevelt, Reagan concluded:

> You and I have a rendezvous with destiny. We can preserve for our children this the last best hope of man on earth or we can sentence them to take the first step into a thousand years of darkness. If we fail, at least let our children and our children's children say of us we justified our brief moment here. We did all that could be done.[53]

Political analysts David Broder and Stephen Hess called the Reagan speech "the most successful national political debut since William Jennings Bryan electrified the 1896 Democratic convention."[54] The speech resonated with conservatives because it was a masterpiece of political fusionism, articulating traditional conservative, libertarian, and anticommunist positions. It provided a conservative answer to the two major problems of modern American history—communism and collectivism—insisting that communism had to be defeated, and that the federal government had become dangerously large and intrusive and had to be rolled back, not managed. While the speech was undoubtedly sacramental, it was at the same time deeply ideological: it was always ideas that motivated Ronald Reagan.

Businessman Henry Salvatori said that he and other leading conservatives would not have approached Reagan to run for governor of California had it not been for his TV talk, titled, "A Time for Choosing."[55] The address immediately raised $1 million for the Goldwater campaign and several more millions from constant rebroadcasts in the following week, and it switched tens of thousands of votes. More than one conservative Republican wished that he had had the chance to vote for Reagan rather than Goldwater, who received only 38.5 percent of the popular vote and carried only six states. California conservatives would soon be given the opportunity.

CHAPTER 4

In the Ring at Last

I N LATE FEBRUARY 1965, a group of influential California Republicans called on Ronald Reagan at his Pacific Palisades home overlooking Los Angeles. All were conservatives, all had raised millions of dollars for the GOP, and all were tired of losing to Democrats. They told Reagan that he was the only person around whom Republicans could rally in the 1966 gubernatorial race, and they were convinced he could defeat Governor Pat Brown. They urged Reagan to travel around the state, find out for himself whether he was acceptable to the party and the people, "and if you are, please, *run*."[1] "I'm an actor, not a politician," he protested, and then admitted that the public reaction to his national telecast for Goldwater the previous October had exceeded anything he had experienced in his movie or TV career. The fifty-four-year-old actor (looking a decade younger) decided to test the political waters of California.[2]

In several ways, he was an ideal candidate for California. He had unquestioned charm and voter appeal. "He is one of the rare men," stated a Los Angeles magazine, "whom other men can stomach even while large groups of women are adoring him."[3] He lived in the more populous southern half of the state—nearly 40 percent of the electorate was located in the greater Los Angeles area. He was assured of substantial financial backing from wealthy Republicans who shared his conservative views. As a former Democrat, he would be able to appeal across partisan lines in a state where party loyalty had always been weak. He was a master of television, a vital medium in a big state with an 840-mile coastline. And according to polls, he was known to 97 percent of California voters.

Reagan made a deal with the governor makers: if they would underwrite his speaking engagements and travel for six months, he would find out for himself whether the people—ordinary people, not Republican partisans—really wanted him to run for governor of California and whether—ever the realist—he had a good chance of winning. The eager visitors readily agreed to his terms and hired the best political campaign team in the state—Stuart Spencer and William Roberts—to manage Reagan's unusual journey into the mind of the California electorate.

At the same time, the prospective candidate was aware that he had to prepare *his* mind for the task ahead. And so, just as he had carefully studied the craft of radio announcing in the early 1930s and then of film acting in the late 1930s, he now undertook to become proficient in a critical part of every campaign, the issues. He was confident he could articulate persuasively his political philosophy—based on limited government and individual responsibility—but he was not familiar with many of California's specific problems and possible solutions.

With his concurrence, Spencer and Roberts closeted him with experts on every imaginable California subject, from redwoods to water to taxes to agriculture. Many were academicians, especially from the University of California at Los Angeles, who presented both sides of an issue and recommended books and monographs for further study. Among the academicians were Stanley Plog of UCLA and Kenneth Holden of San Fernando Valley State College, who said of his "student": "Reagan knows who he is and what he stands for. His library is stacked with books on political philosophy. He can take information and he can assimilate it and use it appropriately in his own words."[4]

It was in mid-October of that year that my wife Anne, who had been active at the top level of New York City politics, and I spent two days traveling with Reagan in Southern California while he considered his political future. I was working on a profile of the new political star for *Reader's Digest*. We were with Reagan early and late—at a Rotary breakfast, at a Kiwanis lunch, at a Republican women's brunch, at an evening address to a businessmen's convention. We saw him dressed in spotless white, dark chocolate brown, and dark blue. We saw worldly women in Armani and Tiffany melt when he looked at them. We saw blasé business leaders jump to their feet applauding when he got through talking about what was right and wrong about America. We saw old pals nudge each other and nod approvingly at his polished performance. We saw little old ladies in tennis shoes from Los Angeles and narrow-tied John Birchers from Orange County line up to shake his hand. He never seemed to get tired or perspire or stop smiling. There was about him the unmistakable aura of a star and of a leader. At the end of the first day, back in our motel, Anne looked at me, and I looked at her, and we both said at the same time, "He's got it!"

Using a Wollensak tape recorder the size of a suitcase, I grilled Reagan on every state and national issue I could think of. He provided a thoughtful answer every time. I asked Reagan how we could prevent future riots like the one in Watts, in which 34 persons, most of them blacks had died, and another 1,032 had been injured. The answer, he said, was not more government money. "Private enterprise has more to offer than Big Brother government," he insisted. "I think that one of these days the [black] must wake up and realize that his supposed friends in court, the Democratic administration . . . [are] simply trying to exchange one odious form of paternalism for another." Why did Watts happen? I asked. It was a combination of things, he replied: a lack of education, frustration over the inability to find a job, leaders who told them there are some laws "that are all right to break. "What else could they expect but what happened?"[5]

If elected, he intended to use the moral power of the governor to defend "state sovereignty" and resist federal encroachment on that sovereignty. "I don't think the federal government can be completely oblivious to a governor," he said, "who will be representing 10 percent of the population of the nation. . . . I think their deeds and actions can be tempered." He acknowledged that such opposition would be difficult because the federal government has "usurped [many] sources of revenues" through federal grants and aid.[6]

Asked about his own beliefs, he quoted from a 1947 interview in which he had said that whether "it comes from management, or labor, or government, or the Right, the Left, or the center, whatever imposes on the freedom of the individual is tyranny and must be opposed. I don't think I have changed from that viewpoint today." Looking back at the Goldwater defeat and considering the dearth of other conservative leaders, I said to Reagan, "In one sense the future of the Republican Party may very well depend on you." He said, "That's a frightening thought."[7] But he was smiling, and didn't seem at all frightened.

At the end of the second day, Reagan took us up the steep winding road to his General Electric home (filled with every possible electrical device but modest in size) for iced tea and cookies. While he and Nancy were in the kitchen, I walked over to the row of bookcases in the library-den and began examining the titles. They were, almost without exception, works of history, economics, and politics, including such conservative classics such as F. A. Hayek's *The Road to Serfdom*, Whittaker Chambers's *Witness*, Henry Hazlitt's *Economics in One Lesson*, and Frederic Bastiat's *The Law*. I opened several books—they were dog eared and underlined, obviously read and more than once. Here was the personal library, not of a shallow actor dangling at the end of someone's strings, but a thinking, reasoning person who had arrived at his conservatism the old-fashioned way—through careful study and serious reflection. That night I wrote in my notebook: "President Reagan?"

We returned to Washington, but Reagan remained on the precampaign trail, winning audiences from San Diego to Redding with his charm, his candor, and his intelligence. After every speech, people lined up to shake his hand and ask, "Why don't you run for governor?" They liked the way he said, "I am not a politician. I am an ordinary citizen with a deep-seated belief that much of what troubles us has been brought about by politicians." It was high time, he suggested, that "more ordinary citizens brought the fresh-air of commonsense thinking to bear on these problems."[8]

When the six months of exploration were nearly over, Reagan came home one night and asked Nancy, "How do you say no to all these people?"[9] At the same time, Reagan realized that if he won the Republican nomination, the mood of Californians was so disgruntled that he had an excellent chance of defeating Pat Brown because of three central issues. Per capita state taxes since 1959, Brown's first year in office, had increased 33 percent. During Brown's tenure, California's population had increased 27 percent while the state budget soared 87 percent. And with 9 percent of the nation's population, California accounted for 17 percent of the nation's crime.

In an interview with the *New York Times*, Reagan reduced his message to one sentence, "I think basically that I stand for what the bulk of Americans stand for—dignity, freedom of the individual, the right to determine your own destiny."[10] There was that essential word again—destiny. His major primary opponent was liberal Republican George Christopher, the two-term mayor of San Francisco. Christopher, despite his unquestioned executive and administrative experience, had serious political flaws. In the words of one reporter, he "looks and talks like a losing television wrestler." Asked why Republicans kept losing elections in California, Christopher replied, "We have straddled the fence with both ears to the ground at the same time too long." And he was careless with facts, implying that Reagan was the candidate of the extremist John Birch Society and at the same time pointing out that Reagan had once belonged to several communist-front organizations—without mentioning that Reagan had broken publicly with the groups when he discovered their Communist roots.

Two issues emerged that Reagan and his team seized upon to pull ahead of Christopher. First, the state's Senate Subcommittee on Un-American Activities accused Clark Kerr, president of the University of California, of having allowed radical students and nonstudents to use the Berkeley campus to become the national "focal point" of the anti–Vietnam War movement. Reagan called on Governor Brown, as president of the university's board of regents, to act immediately "to restore the university to its once high standing."[11] Reagan's willingness to criticize campus radicals and support the war in Vietnam was consistent with conservative principles and was good politics, appealing to social conservatives and patriots of both parties.

Second, the state supreme court, by 5 to 2, overturned Proposition 14, which allowed owners of private property to sell or rent their real estate to whomever they wanted, regardless of race, creed, or color. For Reagan the principle was clear: "the right of a man to dispose of his property or not to dispose of it as he sees fit."[12] Christopher loudly applauded the court's action; Brown was more muted in his approval. He was adding up the issues and the votes, and too many of them were ending up on Reagan's side.

Reagan's one serious misstep in the primary campaign came when he lost his temper in a joint appearance with Christopher at the California convention of the National Negro Republican Assembly. In the question-and-answer period, a delegate criticized Reagan for describing the Civil Rights Act of 1964 as "a bad piece of legislation," causing the conservative, recovering from flu and running a 102-degree temperature, to jump to his feet and say loudly, "I resent the implication that there is any bigotry in my nature." In the ensuing hush, he stalked out of the convention hall.[13]

It was the kind of emotional outburst a neophyte candidate cannot afford. Lasting damage might have been done if Reagan's press secretary, Lyn Nofziger, had not gone after the candidate and bluntly said to him, "We've got to go back. . . . If you don't show they'll think either that you don't like blacks or that you're afraid to face them."[14] Reagan saw immediately that Nofziger was right and returned to the meeting where, at a cocktail party, he received a generally friendly reception, reiterating his personal abhorrence of discrimination and explaining that his opposition to the Civil Rights Act was based on constitutional grounds. When pressed at a news conference about the incident, he quipped, "My wife says I'm very even-tempered."[15] Reagan learned from his mistake: he never again walked out of a political debate.

And he got back to describing his vision of a better California. "What is needed," Reagan declared, "is not *more* government, but *better* government, seeking a solution to the problems that will not add to bureaucracy, or unbalance the budget, or further centralize power." In contrast to Lyndon's Johnson's Great Society, he proposed a Creative Society—"a return to the people of the privilege of self-government, as well as a pledge for more efficient self-government."[16] The idea of self-government—what he called the "God-given freedom to make our own decisions, to plan our own lives and to control our own destiny"—would remain a central theme of Reagan's sixteen years in public office, first as governor and then president.[17]

On primary day, June 7, 1966, Reagan easily won his first political race, defeating Christopher by better than 2 to 1 and carrying 53 of California's 58 counties. He was immediately installed as the favorite to beat Brown in the fall. Analysts used words like *earthquake, landslide,* and *sweeping* as they sought to explain the former actor's debut as a candidate. The liberal magazine, *The Reporter,* quoted Herbert Gold's clever aphorism: Reagan was "Goldwater without fumbles, Nixon without fears, Robert Welch without paranoia, Gary Cooper without awesome stardom." But more to the point, *Newsweek* detected "a new tide of conservatism" in Reagan's startling victory, especially significant now that California would soon supersede New York as the most populous state.[18] Governor Brown ran poorly in the Democratic primary, defeating Los Angeles mayor Sam Yorty by less than 400,000 votes.

As perhaps no other in the union, California was a state of extremes. It had gigantic sprawling Los Angeles county with over 7 million people and tiny Alpine with only four hundred inhabitants. It had Hollywood and Haight-Ashbury, Mount Whitney and Death Valley, the Bank of America and Los Alamos, 182 institutions of higher learning and the Filthy Speech Movement. It led the nation in farm marketing income and was second only to New York in manufacturing. It gave birth to the topless dancer, the topless waitress, and the topless political worker: at the 1964 National

Republican Convention in San Francisco, a voluptuous young woman picked the lobby of the Mark Hopkins Hotel to bare her breasts while the news media fought each other to get pictures. In short, California had a restless, independent, TV-minded electorate of 8 million who liked to confound the pollsters and the politicians—and frequently did.

Nervous Democrats, sensing possible defeat after Reagan's overwhelming win in the Republican primary, released what they called a "profound document," entitled, "Ronald Reagan, Extremist Collaborator—an Exposé." Among the proofs of Reagan's extremism was that he read the conservative weekly *Human Events,* was on the national advisory board of the conservative youth group, Young Americans for Freedom, and had appeared with Dr. Fred Schwarz, whose book, *You Can Trust the Communists (to Be Communists),* was a popular primer on communism.[19]

When the Brown campaign attempted to link Reagan and the John Birch Society (whose leader Robert Welch had written that President Eisenhower was a Communist "stooge" and America was at least 50 percent "communist-controlled"),[20] Reagan released his first and only formal statement about the Birch Society. Reagan denied he had ever been a Bircher and stated he had no intention of becoming one. He reaffirmed his criticism of Welch and his conspiracy theories and urged society members to repudiate their leader's far-fetched ideas. But he pointed out that the FBI had cleared the society (and therefore its members) of subversive activity. He concluded by saying that he had decided not to seek support from "any blocs or groups" but would seek support from individuals "by persuading them to accept my philosophy, not by my accepting theirs." It was, as historian Matthew Dallek has written, a deft and disarming statement that defused the John Birch Society as an issue in just one page.[21]

An unruffled Reagan kept hitting at the Brown administration about high taxes, out-of-control spending, the radical students at Berkeley, and the danger of big government. "Can we possibly believe," he asked over and over, "that anyone can manage our lives better than we can manage them ourselves?"[22] He prudently called for tuition increases at the University of California, warning that the alternative might be a cutback in all of higher education. He asked disenchanted Democrats to support him in order to restore balance to the two-party system in California. And he reiterated that a property owner should have the right to sell or rent to whomever he wanted.

To reassure the electorate and the news media that he was informed on issues important to California, Reagan insisted that a question-and-answer period follow most of his major engagements. He was ready, having assiduously studied for more than a year the material provided him by various academicians and experts. Skeptical reporters waited for Reagan to melt under pressure but came away surprised and impressed. "It was apparent," said one journalist who had been covering him, "that he was not dumb." Indeed, he provided "sensible answers—not just at press conferences, but to audiences."[23]

The Reagan campaign also put together a series of television spots that took the place of many of the usual personal appearances. They were deliberately simple and without gimmicks—just Reagan standing or sitting in front of the camera, talking to the viewers. They worked because Reagan talked about what he believed in and what he believed to be best for California— lower taxes, less spending, greater opportunity for the individual.

Californians listened to what Pat Brown was saying about Reagan— "one of the most dangerous right-wing candidates this country has ever seen"—and then considered the commonsense solutions offered by a calm, confident Reagan, and decided that somebody was very wrong. Reagan consistently appealed to the best in the electorate, suggesting that "we can start a prairie fire that will sweep the nation and prove that we are number one in more than size and crime and taxes." Brown played on the people's worst fears with a thirty-minute film telecast one hundred times throughout the state. Talking to a group of black children, Brown said, "You know, I'm running against an actor . . . and you know who it was who shot Abe Lincoln, don't you?"[24] Democrats made a sixty-second TV spot of this demogogic scene and saturated the state with it in the last week of the campaign.

Ironically, Hollywood got into the act on both sides. Frank Sinatra, Danny Kaye, and Dean Martin entertained at Democratic fund-raising events. (But in 1980, Sinatra attended the Republican National Convention as a guest of Reagan.) GOP events were enlivened by the talents of Walter Brennan and Buddy Ebsen. In numerous interviews, Democrats Kirk Douglas, Burt Lancaster, and Gene Kelly questioned Reagan's ability to govern while Republicans Pat Boone, Roy Rogers, and John Wayne expressed confidence in Reagan's political abilities on television and radio.

In this campaign, Matthew Dallek wrote, Reagan was a dream candidate—quick with a sound bite (pledging a "moral crusade" to end the "arrogance" of the Brown administration, speaking of the need for "commonsense" government), able to give confident answers to reporters' questions, willing to listen to advisers who helped forge positions on critical issues such as taxes, higher education, poverty, and crime. In a broader sense, he was also helped by the decline of traditional American liberalism, the rise of the radical New Left, and the emergence of a formidable conservative movement. But at the core of every one of his campaigns, from the very first in 1966 when he ran as a "citizen politician" to his last in 1984 when he sought reelection as president, was Reagan's philosophical commitment to smaller government and a firm anticommunism.[25]

On Monday, November 7, Reagan spoke at large airport rallies in six cities; four days earlier, he had been covered with confetti and cheered by thousands during a parade in San Francisco, Pat Brown's hometown. On that last day, the candidate cautioned the sign-waving crowds against overconfidence—the prestigious *Los Angeles Times* had endorsed Reagan the day before—and urged them to turn out in full force on the morrow. They did. Reagan trounced Brown by 1 million votes, winning 57 percent to 42 percent in the popular vote. Republicans won every major state office but one, reduced the Democratic majorities in the assembly and state senate to razor-thin margins, and picked up three seats in the U.S. House of Representatives. Several thousand campaign workers and supporters jammed the Biltmore Bowl election night for a victory celebration. Some enthusiasts unfurled a huge "Reagan for President" banner, causing the governor-elect at a news conference the next day to disavow any presidential ambitions.

Reagan discovered that the departing Pat Brown had left him a Herculean task, indeed several of them. There was a gap of $500 million between revenues and expenditures in the general fund, and under its constitution, California is required to balance its budget. Governor Reagan ordered all state agencies to implement a 10 percent reduction in their operations (the overall savings would eventually total about 8 percent of operating expenses) and warned that a tax increase was inevitable. The new administration cut expenses wherever it could and then cut them again, selling the state Convair airplane used by Brown; banning expensive colored brochures and pamphlets by departments; reducing the state civil service by 1.5 percent; and eliminating $750,000 for a new governor's mansion.

In March, Governor Reagan submitted a 1967–1968 budget of $5.06 billion—the largest state budget in U.S. history—providing relief to property taxpayers and covering unexpected increases in Medi-Cal costs, the state's cooperative program with federal Medicare. Reagan was keeping a campaign promise with the aid to property owners and was determined to provide reasonable medical care for those truly in need. The budget increase was the smallest in years—about 8 percent over the preceding year—but still required a gigantic tax increase of $946 million, again the largest state tax bill in U.S. history. "The people of California are still paying too much for government," Reagan acknowledged, "but I'm optimistic that in the next year we can reduce the cost of government."[26]

The California Record

A pattern was established in Reagan's first year as governor that he followed throughout his two terms in Sacramento: cut and trim government wherever possible, keep income and outgo in balance as required by law, use business and professional experts to make government more efficient, and be prepared to make unpopular decisions if necessary. Early in the administration, Reagan aides circulated a single sheet to appointees expressing the governor's political philosophy which—political scientists Gary G. Hamilton and Nicole Woolsey Biggart correctly state—he expected members of his administration to follow as closely as he did.

Governor's Philosophy

- Keep the size and cost of government as small as possible.
- Solve problems and perform governmental functions at the lowest possible level.
- Avoid the creation of additional layers of government.
- Government should not perform a function that can be effectively performed by the private sector.
- Promote innovative and creative approaches to governmental programs.
- Utilize the skills and experience of the private sector in carrying out governmental programs.
- Federal government should communicate and administer its programs through the state government to local governments.
- Government exists to protect us from each other. No government on earth can possibly afford to protect us from ourselves.[27]

When Ronald Reagan took the office of governor in January 1967, California was spending a million dollars more each day than it was taking in. When he left office in December 1974, he turned over to his successor a surplus of $554 million. Under Reagan, California's bonds were upgraded to the highest possible rating—Moody's Triple-A—for the first time in thirty-one years. "We exaggerate very little," editorialized the *San Francisco Examiner,* "when we say that [Reagan] has saved the state from bankruptcy."[28]

Reagan was the biggest tax-cutter in the state's history, enacting over $5.7 billion in tax relief, despite the almost $1 billion tax increase in his first year. His measures included the first comprehensive property tax relief program in California history, the elimination of taxes on families earning less than $8,000 a year, the reduction of taxes on lower-to-middle wage earners, and reduction of the business inventory tax by half. "California is in good financial shape today," stated the veteran legislative analyst A. Alan Post, "because Reagan gave it a sound tax base."[29]

Reagan climaxed his tax limitation efforts in 1973 by sponsoring Proposition 1, an amendment to the state constitution that would have eventually placed a ceiling of 7 percent on the income tax that the state could levy on its citizens. Although the measure lost—gaining 46 percent of the vote despite fierce opposition by Democrats and liberal special interest groups—columnist M. Stanton Evans wrote that Proposition 1 "spawned a series of parallel efforts in twenty other states."[30] With the success of Howard Jarvis's Proposition 13 in 1978 in California and passage of similar laws in twelve other states that year, Reagan's 1973 initiative can be legitimately called the birth of the tax limitation movement in America.

Due to inflation (a 44 percent increase during his tenure) and a usually Democratic legislature, the state's annual budget more than doubled during Reagan's eight years as governor, from $4.6 billion to $10.2 billion. Another major reason for the increase was the new or expanded programs mandated by the U.S. Congress or the state legislature. A fairer criterion of spending is the state's operations budget which increased by about 50 percent from 1967 to 1974—by comparison, New York spending almost tripled during the same span. At the same time, the size of state government as measured by the number of employees was held to a near standstill. A determined Reagan resisted the spenders all the way, vetoing 994 bills—only one veto was overridden. "There is solid evidence," wrote the *Los Angeles Times,* "that Reagan, particularly through his vetoes, [was] an effective brake in keeping government spending from accelerating at an even more rapid rate."[31]

Reagan's determination to resist spending was tested when the California legislature voted a large increase in public education funds, mostly for increases in teachers' salaries. Director of Finance Caspar Weinberger and others recommended that the governor veto the measure, alarming one political adviser who warned Reagan, "Governor, you cannot veto a teacher salary increase. You'll never get reelected if you do." To which Reagan quietly replied, "But I did not come here to get reelected." He vetoed the bill, held the line on expenditures, and was reelected.[32]

Although liberal critics and even friendly conservatives like Dinesh D'Souza have described Reagan's first term as "undistinguished," a more reasonable finding is that he set the stage for his later tax cuts by first balancing the books, delivered on his law and order promises by restoring the death penalty for capital crimes and providing stiffer penalties against such crimes as rape and robbery, instituted tuition at the state university system, created the first state department of consumer affairs in the country, and laid the political foundation for his reelection in 1970. He also established a decision-making process that was similar to that of another prominent Republican—President Eisenhower. As a rule, Reagan made no important decision without first discussing it in detail at a cabinet meeting and then seeking and obtaining consensus.

To help the process, William Clark, Reagan's first chief of staff, created the one-page memorandum which was divided into four parts: issues, facts, discussion (pro and con), and recommendation. At first, Clark acknowledged, there were frequent objections that complicated topics could not be so condensed. But it was found, Clark told me, "that almost any issue can be reduced to a single page. If the governor wanted to go into more depth, he would request more detailed reports. He's a late-night reader." To those who criticized the system, Clark had a ready reply: "Everyone wants to see the governor, but the only way he can operate efficiently is to ration his time. Otherwise, chaos would exist."[33] Edwin Meese III, who succeeded Clark as chief of staff in February 1969, retained the one-page memo—and brought it with him to Washington when he became counselor to President Reagan in the White House.

As governor, Reagan normally followed a 9 A.M. to 5:30 P.M. schedule, often saying to his aides as he walked out, "Hey, guys, get out. Go home to your wives."[34] His relaxed approach helped reduce the pressure on his staff, enabling them to work more efficiently if far past Reagan's quitting time. At the same time, as William Clark and others have confirmed, Reagan conscientiously read before going to bed every report and background memo given him. His work schedule was consistent with his philosophy of concentrating on the most important items on the governor's agenda and not being distracted by the less important. He rejected the compulsive micromanaging style of Richard Nixon and Jimmy Carter, famous, when he was president, for overseeing the playing schedule of the White House tennis courts. Reagan's theory of administration, Lou Cannon wrote, was sound. He believed in hiring people of proven ability who drew upon the available expertise "while nudging the bureaucracy in the direction he wanted it to go."[35]

Although not given to sitting up all night drinking and trading stories with politicians of either party, Reagan recognized the importance of timely, low-key lobbying. In his first year as governor, he and Nancy invited small groups of state legislators and their wives to dine at the governor's residence. After dinner, the gentlemen would retire downstairs to a large recreation room where Reagan would take off his tux and run a gigantic electric train while others played pool or sang songs around an upright piano. After such an evening, it was difficult for legislators to think of the governor as an extremist or a know-nothing—in fact, several liberal Democrats conceded they liked him.[36]

One legislative action of Reagan's that no amount of lobbying could persuade conservatives to applaud was his signing the most liberal abortion law in America. In June 1967, six years before the Supreme Court's *Roe v. Wade* decision, the California legislature passed a bill allowing abortion where the life or the physical or mental health of the mother was endangered and if the pregnancy was the result of rape or incest. Opponents warned that the health exception was drawn so broadly that it amounted to abortion on demand. The governor publicly expressed his reservations, particularly about a section dealing with the birth of a potentially deformed child. "I cannot justify morally," he said, "taking of the unborn life simply on the supposition that it is going to be less than a perfect human being, because I don't see very far . . . from that to some day deciding after birth that we will sort out those people who should be allowed to live or not; and I don't see any difference between that and what Hitler tried to do."[37]

Nevertheless, Reagan signed the bill—and came to regret his action, deeply. The number of legal abortions in California soared from 518 in 1967 to an average of 100,000 between 1968 and 1974. When legislators in 1970 proposed new liberalizations in the abortion law, Reagan successfully opposed them. In a "Dear Citizen" letter, he said: "Those who summarily advocate a *blanket population control* [Reagan's emphasis] should think carefully. Who might they be doing away? Another Lincoln, or Beethoven, an Einstein or an Edison? Who shall play God?"[38] As a 1976 presidential candidate, he said of his signing the California abortion bill, "I wouldn't make the same mistake again." He said that he "did more soul-searching and studying on the subject than anything else in my eight years" as governor. He emphasized that he now opposed abortion in all circumstances except when a mother's life was imperiled by her pregnancy—a position he maintained as a candidate in 1980 and throughout his eight years as president. He summed up his strong feelings in a letter: "If, with pregnancy, a window appeared in a woman's body so that she could look at her own child develop, I wonder at what point she would decide it was all right to kill it."[39]

Most observers are agreed that Reagan's most impressive achievement as governor of California was the adoption of a far-reaching welfare reform program. By 1971, the annual cost of the state's welfare system was an alarming $3 billion. The welfare caseload was increasing at a rate of up to forty thousand people a month and totaled 2.3 million that spring. In response to the crisis, Reagan formed the Welfare Reform Task Force, coordinated by chief of staff Ed Meese, that put together a program that became law and ultimately transformed public welfare not only in California but throughout the nation. Many of its provisions were included in the historic welfare reform act passed by the U.S. Congress a quarter of a century later.

Among the changes: penalties were stiffened for welfare fraud; recipients with jobs were removed from the welfare rolls when their outside income exceeded 150 percent of their basic needs; adult children were required to contribute to the support of their aged parents on welfare; the power of counties to make absent fathers pay for the support of their families was broadened; and able-bodied recipients were required to take job training or work on public works projects at least four hours a day.

The results in California were dramatic. By September 1974, the total caseload had dropped by approximately 20 percent, but benefits to those without any outside income had risen by 43 percent. The dollar savings in the first two years were an estimated $1 billion. Even Reagan's Democratic successor, Jerry Brown, was impressed, commenting, "Considering today's high unemployment, it is amazing that [the Reagan welfare program] has kept welfare down as much as it has."[40]

The Democratic legislature, dominated by liberals beholden to the welfare establishment, strongly resisted the proposed changes. But Reagan asked the people through a series of television and radio programs to let their legislators know how they felt about reducing the number of people on welfare but increasing the support for those who really needed help. One day, Assembly Speaker Robert Moretti appeared at Governor Reagan's door and, holding up his hands, said, "Stop the cards and letters. I'm ready to negotiate a welfare reform act."[41] California's balanced approach to welfare was so effective that even liberal Republican governor Nelson Rockefeller adopted it for New York.

Reagan's welfare reform, summed up veteran conservative analyst Allan H. Ryskind, "proved that conservative principles applied to a seemingly intractable domestic problem could be highly effective." The measure's success helped transform Reagan from a celebrity governor grounded in conservative philosophy into "a high-performing chief of state and a credible presidential candidate."[42]

Campus unrest was born on the Berkeley campus of the University of California in 1964 with the so-called Free Speech Movement. Once in office, Governor Reagan acted decisively to quell the lawlessness, tightening laws against unlawful assembly, suspending state financial support of students convicted of campus disturbances, and making it a crime to coerce the officials or teachers of any educational institution. Reagan emphasized that he was not seeking to deny academic freedom to anyone but to protect the rights of the law-abiding majority on campus. "Preservation of free speech," he said sternly, "does not justify letting beatniks and advocates of sexual orgies, drug usage and 'filthy speech' disrupt the academic community and interfere with our universities' purpose of learning and research."[43] In the spring of 1969, following the fire bombing of Wheeler Hall at Berkeley, the vandalizing of a dozen buildings, and the discovery of fire bombs, Reagan acceded to the request of the school administration and declared a state of emergency. "I am duty bound," he explained, "to make available all the force at my command to protect the rights of the people"—including the right of teachers and students "to learn without fear of violence or threat of violence."[44]

As a result, while Columbia, Cornell, the University of Wisconsin, and other schools were erupting in 1969 and 1970, experiencing widespread destruction and even deaths, almost all California campuses remained open because of Reagan's firmness and that of college presidents like S. I. Hayakawa of San Francisco State University. At the same time, Reagan did not stint legitimate education funding, considering it an important investment in the state's future. During the eight years of the Reagan administration, for example, aid to the state university system rose 105.5 percent while support for the primary and secondary school system similarly increased 105 percent.

Reagan worked hard to reverse the trend to centralized authority over K–12 education by encouraging the joint cooperation of teachers, parents, and local school boards. He revised teacher tenure law, making it possible to weed out incompetent teachers, signed legislation prohibiting school busing for any purpose without the written permission of the parents, enacted a law requiring textbooks to be available for public display and inspection before adoption, and required parental involvement in the development of sex education courses. But he did not attempt any fundamental reform of lower education, in deference to California's constitutionally and independently elected superintendent of public instruction. He thereby disappointed those parents, wrote public policy consultant Charles D. Hobbs, who wanted "to see their children learn to read, write, add, and subtract as well as the children in Ohio or Virginia or any of about twenty other states."[45]

To the surprise of many African Americans and Hispanics, minorities were not ignored by the Reagan administration. One-fifth of Reagan's first one hundred appointments were minority citizens. He appointed the first black ever to head a California department as well as numerous minority community members to policy-making posts on boards, commissions, and the judiciary. He named more Hispanics to key state positions than any governor before him. Wilson Riles, elected State Superintendent of Public Instruction in 1970 and therefore California's highest-ranking black official, said that he expected to have problems with Reagan but later admitted that the governor had given him "full access"—he was "always receptive" to hearing an opposing view and "sometimes even willing" to accept it.[46]

Opposed to throwing government money at a problem, Reagan worked to strengthen private business in minority areas and to increase educational opportunities for blacks and other minorities. He developed a State Plan for Employment Opportunity, under which jobs for minority youths would be significantly increased. He signed legislation—the first of its type in the nation—providing tax incentives to private lending institutions to make real estate loans in low-income families in inner city neighborhoods. He significantly expanded bilingual study programs to assist Hispanic students' proficiency in English.

As an admirer of the "other" Roosevelt—Theodore—and his pro-environment policies, Reagan approved the toughest antismog laws in the country and the strongest water pollution control law in U.S. history. A total of 145,000 acres, including forty-one miles of ocean frontage, were added to the state park system. At the same time, he vetoed a bill that would have practically eliminated the internal combustion engine, and he opposed regulations of the Environmental Protection Agency that would have brought major social and economic disruption in the state.

Some think that Reagan's finest hour as governor came in 1972 on the issue of the Dos Rios dam, a proposed 730-foot structure on the Middle Fork of the Eel River, one of California's few remaining wild rivers. Both the Army Corps of Engineers and the state water bureaucracy favored the dam—almost everyone assumed that a decision in favor of the dam was a foregone conclusion. But Norman Livermore, Reagan's director of resources, and a few conservationists pointed out that a historic valley would have been flooded by the dam along with the gravesites of the Yuki Indian tribe. The Yukis argued that their graves and some of the valley was theirs by treaty. "We've broken too damn many treaties," an aroused Reagan explained, rejecting the Dos Rios dam while signing the Wild and Scenic Rivers Act. "We're not going to flood them out."[47]

Although the conduct of U.S. foreign policy was rarely a major issue during his years in Sacramento, Reagan still articulated when he could his strong anticommunism and his suspicion of accommodation with the Soviet Union, as during the annual Captive Nations Week. More and more, he noted, "we have diluted that theme until now we use the [week] to speak of peace with no mention of freedom. Is it possible that while we are sorry for the captives, we do not want to offend the captors?" On Vietnam, he favored a sharp escalation of the war to "win as quickly as possible" and to let the military recommend how to win it.[48] Addressing the Young Republican National Convention in June 1967, he set forth the "peace through strength" theme that served as the core of his foreign policy as president. We should "deal" with the communists, he said, but only "through a position of strength, not relying on the hope that an enemy, increasingly able to match us in power, will just one day undergo a change of heart and give up his Marxist dream."[49]

Californians liked Reagan's notion of limited government and individual responsibility, and reelected him in 1970, giving him a popular vote margin of 500,000 votes. *Newsweek* described Reagan as "one of the most brilliantly gifted politicians anywhere in the U.S. today—a campaigner unmatched for sheer star quality since the departure of Dwight Eisenhower and the arrival of the Kennedys a decade ago." At fifty-nine, wrote *Life*'s Paul O'Neill, Reagan is "a tall, tanned and handsome figure in immaculate white linen and beautifully cut dark suits who moves as easily as an athlete." And he had the quality, reminiscent of FDR and John F. Kennedy, to make "a listener his partner." Veteran political reporter James M. Perry acknowledged the formidable mind behind the handsome "facade," writing that Reagan was "intelligent . . . shrewd . . . and proud of" being a conservative. Jesse Unruh, defeated by Reagan in his reelection bid, paid grudging tribute to his opponent: "As a governor, I think he has been better than most Democrats would concede. . . . As a politician, I think he has been nearly masterful."[50]

Assessing Reagan's governorship, a *Los Angeles Times* analyst wrote dismissively that Reagan had left footprints on the government of California that "can be swept away as easily as if he had walked on sand." But Lou Cannon, a former political correspondent for a leading California newspaper as well as the *Washington Post,* arrived at a far different conclusion: "Reagan set a tone of skepticism about liberal, expansionist government that persists to this day in California." From a standing start as a political novice, Cannon pointed out, Reagan "mastered the intricacies of governing the nation's most populous and macroscopic state." He proved as no one had before him that it was possible "to succeed as governor of a major state without abandoning conservative principles." Furthermore, wrote Cannon, Reagan carried his doctrine of limited government "to the national political state, from which he tugged the nation in a conservative direction."[51]

The Reagan administration in California spanned turbulent times that included unprecedented inflation and two recessions, domestic violence over the Vietnam War and frequent campus uprisings, unrest in the inner cities, and Watergate. Through it all Reagan pursued a policy of "squeeze, cut and trim" state spending that kept California's taxes and spending from soaring into the stratosphere as they had under Pat Brown and previous governors and still enabled his administration to provide essential services. At the same time, he made first-class appointments to the bench and set a high moral standard matched by those who served under him—there was no "Scam" or "Gate" during the Reagan years. If he was not as conservative as some wished (state senator John Schmitz, a member of the John Birch Society, scornfully called Reagan "the great compromiser"), he nevertheless pioneered the anti–big government movement that emerged as a central issue in the national politics of 1976 and has remained one ever since.[52]

And what does a masterful politician do after he has been the successful governor of the most populous state in the union—particularly if he believes that the future of the country and of the world is in doubt?

CHAPTER 5

The Biggest Role of All

SIX MONTHS AFTER LEAVING THE GOVERNOR'S HOUSE in Sacramento and in supposed retirement, Reagan was broadcasting a five-times-a-week radio commentary on several hundred radio stations, writing a weekly column for some two hundred newspapers, making speeches from Los Angeles to Miami, and proclaiming (at a conservative dinner in Washington, D.C.) that the Republican Party must raise a philosophical banner "of bold colors and no pale pastels."[1] Everyone at the dinner knew he was referring to the increasingly soft policies of President Gerald Ford, at home and abroad.

Reagan was concerned about the $50 billion deficit that the Ford administration had incurred as well as Ford's avid pursuit of détente, including the adoption of the SALT II accords and his plan to turn the Panama Canal over to Panamanian dictator Omar Torrijos. Still he did not relish running against an incumbent Republican president, even an appointed one. Seeing himself "as a party unifier, not a party divider," he hesitated about declaring his candidacy as he had once before.[2]

Reagan made a very belated bid for the 1968 Republican presidential nomination, delaying his formal announcement until the national convention actually opened in Miami. Almost coyly, he explained that "the office seeks the man, the man doesn't seek the office." Reagan waited in a trailer outside the convention hall while campaign manager F. Clifton White brought the Florida delegation to see him. Some of the women delegates wept because they wanted to vote for Reagan but were bound to Richard Nixon. When Reagan made a last minute fervent appeal to conservative Senator Strom Thurmond of South Carolina, the veteran legislator replied: "Son, you'll be president some day, but this isn't your year." Thurmond, like almost every other major officeholder, had already been locked up by Nixon and his supraefficient organization.[3]

Nixon won the presidential nomination on the first ballot with 692 votes while Governor Rockefeller received 299 delegate votes and Reagan was a distant third with 182 votes. Even so it was an impressive showing by a man who had been governor barely eighteen months. "Because Reagan came very close to unraveling Nixon's majority strength in the South," wrote *Human Events,* he forced Nixon to issue assurances to Thurmond, John Tower of Texas, and other conservatives that he would "guide the Republican Party in a starboard direction. Thus, even in losing," the conservative weekly newspaper pointed out, "Reagan managed to win a victory for conservatism."[4]

Seven years later, he was willing to admit that in some instances the man must seek the office. He allowed an old political friend, Senator Paul Laxalt of Nevada, to form an exploratory "Citizens for Reagan" committee, and in November 1975, he announced that he was a candidate for the Republican presidential nomination, stating:

> The American dream has somewhere been mislaid. We have to hope and believe the loss is temporary. Millions of Americans across this land still live by that dream and are determined to keep and expand their freedom and independence. They know that to do this they must reduce the power centralized in Washington

A turning point for Reagan had been Ford's refusal to meet with famed Russian dissident and author Alexander Solzhenitsyn. Reagan ridiculed the reasons given by the Ford White House: the president had to attend a party for his daughter; the Russian writer had not formally requested a meeting; it was not clear "what [the president] would gain by a meeting with Solzhenitsyn." Reagan made it clear that a President Reagan would have been honored to sit down with the famed survivor and chronicler of the Gulag Archipelago.[5]

Trying to calculate his chances against President Ford, Reagan must have been encouraged by the considered opinion of the *Washington Post*'s David Broder, perhaps the most respected political reporter in Washington, who wrote that Republican activists "crave someone whose philosophy they know and trust." Broder expressed the "hunch" that if Reagan ran "in support of the conservative principles he's been talking about all these years, it just might be one heck of a horse race."[6] And Reagan was able to take satisfaction from the blistering attack by the *Daily World,* the official publication of the U.S. Communist Party, which described his candidacy as "racist" and "the strongest drive for the Presidency by ultra-Right business and political forces, both inside and outside the Republican party orbit, since the Presidential candidacy of Sen. Barry Goldwater in 1964."[7]

The conservative challenger was an early favorite in New Hampshire, site of the first Republican primary, with the enthusiastic backing of Governor Meldrim Thomson, publisher William Loeb of the influential *Manchester Union-Leader,* and other key conservatives in the state. But the Ford people zeroed in on a Reagan proposal (drafted by research director Jeffrey Bell) to transfer some $90 billion worth of federal programs to the states, including education, public housing and community development, revenue sharing, and certain health and welfare programs. Ford operatives charged that state and local tax rates would have to be hiked to cover the cost of the transferred programs. (Reagan later disavowed the $90 billion figure but stood by the federalist principle of transferring federal programs to state and local governments.) The Ford campaign also suggested that if elected president, Reagan would slash social security, veterans' benefits, and other welfare programs.

Reagan was placed on the defensive and was kept there by an overly protective campaign staff headed by campaign manager John Sears, a Nixon pragmatist who constantly sought to mute Reagan's conservatism. Fearful of mishaps, Sears pulled Reagan out of New Hampshire the weekend before the primary election, neglecting to tell the candidate that his once-comfortable lead had vanished. On primary day, a disappointed Reagan received 48 percent of the popular vote to Ford's 49.4 percent and lost New Hampshire by a wafer-thin 1,587 votes. Reagan's showing against a sitting president was impressive (better than Eugene McCarthy's 42 percent against Lyndon Johnson in the 1968 Democratic primary which had helped persuade LBJ not to seek reelection) but could not erase the perception he had been expected to win.

President Ford rode the momentum he gained in New Hampshire to win succeeding GOP primaries in Massachusetts, Vermont, Illinois (Reagan's native state), and Florida, establishing himself as the undisputed frontrunner by mid-March. Campaigning in North Carolina alongside Republican Governor James Holshouser, an overconfident Ford declared he didn't care whether Reagan remained in the presidential primary race or dropped out— he was "going to Kansas City [site of the August GOP national convention] and getting the nomination." A grimly determined Reagan, backed by Republican Senator Jesse Helms, responded that he was "in this race all the way" and stepped up his attacks on Ford's gingerly handling of the Soviet Union and "the greatest budget deficit in the nation's history."[8]

In North Carolina, wrote Lou Cannon, Reagan had reached a point in his political career as critical as when he gave his electrifying television speech for Goldwater in October 1964. Without "A Time for Choosing," Reagan would not have been catapulted into the first ranks of American politics nor would he have been entreated to run for governor of California by Holmes Tuttle, Henry Salvatori, and other influential Republicans. Without a victory in the North Carolina primary, Reagan would have been jettisoned, however reluctantly, by conservatives looking for a winner and would have faded from view like so many other also-rans in American politics.

Understanding what was at stake, Reagan responded as he usually did in a time of testing, drawing on inner reserves of strength and faith. He went on the offensive against Ford's foreign policy, his domestic policy, and his cabinet, particularly Secretary of State Henry Kissinger. He mocked the president's extravagant use of the patronage power of the White House. "I understand Mr. Ford has arrived in the state," Reagan said the Saturday before the primary. "If he comes here with the same list of goodies as he did in Florida, the band won't know whether to play 'Hail to the Chief' or 'Santa Claus Is Coming to Town.'"[9]

Despite the large, enthusiastic crowds and other signs that Reagan was turning things around in the state, reporters kept asking him when he would quit. On election day, when they pressed him, Reagan replied that he intended to continue campaigning, win or lose. When they persisted, he refused to answer, saying he would respond only to other questions. There was a long moment of silence before someone ended the impasse with a question on another subject. It was this kind of determination that was among the more important reasons why "Reagan eventually became president of the United States."[10]

Following Reagan's 54 percent to 46 percent upset of Ford in the North Carolina primary, everyone including the president acknowledged that the nature of the 1976 Republican presidential nomination race had been fundamentally altered: there was a real race. Postprimary polls revealed that voters liked Reagan's emphasis on the need for a sturdy foreign policy. Secretary of State Henry Kissinger, Reagan charged, "thinks the day of the

U.S. has passed, and today is the day of the Soviet Union."[11] Of those who agreed with Reagan that the United States had become militarily inferior to the Soviet Union under the Ford administration, about 80 percent voted for the challenger. Of those who disagreed that the United States was number two, about 80 percent voted for the president. Reagan was also helped in North Carolina by a low turnout of about 40 percent, lower than in the earlier GOP primaries he lost.

Like two heavyweights standing in the middle of the ring and trading their best punches, Reagan and Ford each won key primaries in the following four months. Challenger Reagan took Texas, Indiana, Georgia, Missouri, and, the biggest prize of all, California—often with the help of thousands of Democratic and Independent votes. President Ford captured his home state of Michigan, Maryland, Kentucky, Tennessee, New Jersey, and Ohio. The media played up the horserace nature of the campaign, but something far more important was occurring—a seismic shift in American politics. Former Democrat Reagan was forging a new majority of Republicans, Democrats, and Independents under the Republican banner. A special target was the Wallace Democrats to whom Reagan offered something to vote for, not against. Both Reagan and outsider Jimmy Carter were doing well, wrote analyst Richard Whalen, because they were "perceived as unsullied by Watergate, untainted by Vietnam, and uncorrupted by a Washington system that isn't working."[12]

For those who wanted to know what a President Reagan would seek to accomplish in his first one hundred days, *Conservative Digest* published an exclusive interview I conducted with the candidate in his Los Angeles home. Among the highlights: Reagan would focus on the fact that Washington (i.e., the federal government) was "trying to do things that Washington should not be doing." Like Roosevelt with his fireside chats, he would go to the people to get their support to make the necessary changes in the way government operated. He would let the Soviets know that "we're not going to accept number two, we do accept the leadership of the free world, and we're going to stand by our allies" like Taiwan and South Korea. He would appoint task forces on everything from the civil service to welfare, seeking to make the government the true servant of the people. And he would seek to form a New Majority coalition of Republicans and Democrats to help him carry out "the politics of common sense."[13]

By mid-July 1976 and the end of the primary season, the delegate count was extraordinarily close: Ford led with just under 1,100 delegates while Reagan closely trailed with a little more than 1,000. A total of 1,130 delegates was needed for nomination. In a calculated last-minute attempt to gain uncommitted delegates, campaign manager John Sears persuaded Reagan to name moderate senator Richard Schweiker of Pennsylvania as his running mate. Seemingly disparate in philosophy and background, Reagan and Schweiker had much in common. Both were strongly anti-abortion and shared many of the same social concerns about the decline of the family and the community. Both were strong Christians: Schweiker was Catholic and the father of five. "I'm not a knee-jerk liberal," Schweiker said during a six hour get-acquainted session with Reagan, who responded, "And I'm not a knee-jerk conservative."[14] The Schweiker gambit, however, failed to move any delegates into the Reagan column, and the final agonizingly close tally was 1,187 for Ford, 1,070 for Reagan—a difference of only 117 delegates. Selecting Schweiker demonstrated Reagan's willingness to be flexible in his tactics in achieving a goal. Four years later, he was agreeable to having George Bush, his leading primary opponent and the favorite of the Republican establishment, as his vice president.

On the final evening of the national convention in Kansas City, after Ford had given his numbingly earnest acceptance address, he waved for Reagan to join him on the podium. Reluctant at first, Reagan finally gave in and appeared, tall, relaxed, "improbably handsome," in the words of one observer.[15] Without notes or teleprompter, he gave an eloquent six-minute speech that had thousands of delegates and guests and a national television audience of millions spellbound as he suggested what would have been a major goal of his presidency—arms reduction rather than arms control. After noting that the party had adopted a platform of "bold, unmistakable colors with no pale, pastel shades" and criticizing the Democrats for their wayward ways, he began to tell a story (who better than a master story-teller?) about being asked to write a letter about the major issues of the day for a time capsule to be opened in a hundred years.

Reagan spoke of the domestic problems confronting America, "the erosion of freedom that has taken place under Democrat rule in this country, the invasion of private rights, the controls and restrictions on the vitality of the great free economy that we enjoy." And he spoke of the world "in which the great powers have poised and aimed at each other horrible missiles of destruction, nuclear weapons, that can in a matter of minutes arrive at each other's country and destroy, virtually, the civilized world we live in."

He said that whether Americans a hundred years hence will "have the freedoms that we have known up until now will depend on what we do here." "Will they look back, he asked, and say, 'Thank God for those people in 1976 who headed off that loss of freedom, who kept us now a hundred years later free, who kept our world from nuclear destruction'?" "This is our challenge," he concluded, his voice low and resonant, and why "we must go forth from here united, determined that what a great general said a few years ago is true: there is no substitute for victory, Mr. President."[16]

There was a spontaneous roar of approbation from the delegates—from those who had been for Reagan and those who had backed Ford but wondered if they had nominated the wrong man. "Beautiful, just beautiful," Vice President Rockefeller was heard to say as he grasped Reagan's hand.[17] TV cameras vainly searched the convention hall for a dry eye.

Reagan himself had been close to tears earlier in the day when he talked to his anguished campaign staffers. "Don't get cynical," he said to them. "Don't give up your ideals. . . . Recognize that there are millions and millions of Americans out there who want what you want . . . a shining city on a hill."[18] "We lost," Reagan acknowledged to advisers and workers, many of whom were weeping, "but the cause—the cause goes on." And then he added a couple of lines from an old Scottish ballad, "I'll lay me down and bleed awhile; though I am wounded, I am not slain. I shall rise and fight again."[19]

Reporters and politicians alike agreed that his talk had been movingly delivered, but then added that it was almost certainly the final curtain speech of a defeated and aged candidate. After all, Ronald Reagan would be *sixty-nine* if he chose to run again in 1980—making him the oldest candidate for the presidency in American history. The experts did not pay sufficient attention to Reagan's other words that mournful morning: "Nancy and I," he emphasized, "we aren't going to go back and sit in a rocking chair and say, 'Well, that's all for us.'"[20] Two of his closest aides, Michael Deaver and Lyn Nofziger, were convinced he would not run again.

Unbeknownst to them, Reagan was thinking about 1980 on the flight back home from Kansas City. He viewed his failure to win the presidential nomination as part of God's plan for him. "Bearing what we cannot change," he wrote a supporter, "going on with what God has given us, confident there is a destiny, somehow seems to bring a reward we wouldn't exchange for any other." And then Reagan added these revealing words: "It takes a lot of fire and heat to make a piece of steel."[21] Reagan's desire to run again would be fueled by the mounting failures of the Carter administration.

"We Win and They Lose"

In January 1977, following Ford's disappointing loss to Carter—one highlight was Ford's inexplicable remark in a television debate that "there is no Soviet dominance of Eastern Europe"[22]—Richard V. Allen, one of the conservative movement's top foreign policy experts, called on Ronald Reagan in Los Angeles. Allen wanted Reagan to support his candidacy for governor of New Jersey, Allen's home state. Reagan readily agreed, offering to sign some fund-raising letters, and then asked Allen to spend "some time" with him, discussing foreign policy and national defense. For the next several hours, the two men "circled" the globe, analyzing such major issues as U.S.-Soviet relations and the theory of Mutual Assured Destruction (MAD). "I had never heard," Allen later recalled, "a major politician dissect the failings of those flawed policies of Nixon and Ford so skillfully."[23]

At last Reagan said that he would like to tell Allen his theory of the Cold War: "Some say that I am 'simplistic,' but I believe that many complex problems have simple answers. So about the Cold War: My view is that we win and they lose." Allen was stunned but inspired: "If you mean it, and if you are going to run for president again, you can count me in." Reagan did mean it because he believed that America was stronger than the Soviets, that it was more flexible, imaginative, and just, and that it could "integrate its economic, technological, capital and moral resources to emerge the victor."[24] Here in its embryonic form was what would become known as the Reagan Doctrine.

The lengthy meeting with Dick Allen (who abandoned his plan to run for New Jersey governor and became Reagan's primary foreign policy adviser) underscored the seriousness with which Reagan approached the 1980 campaign. In 1975, before his run against Ford, Reagan had prepared "to be a candidate" but from 1977 through 1979, wrote historian Stephen Hayward, he prepared "to be president."[25] There were trips to London, Berlin, and Paris, under Allen's guidance, where he met conservative political leaders such as Margaret Thatcher and Helmut Kohl. From his office at the Hoover Institution, economist Martin Anderson began forming a formidable network of issue task forces for the as-yet-undeclared candidate. By

Election Day 1980, the Reagan campaign had signed up 461 experts for forty-eight different task forces—including such heavyweights as Milton Friedman, Alan Greenspan, George Shultz, and Jeane Kirkpatrick.

During the mid- and late seventies, Reagan familiarized himself with a remarkably wide range of domestic and foreign issues while doing the research for his daily radio commentary. Surrounded by newspaper and magazine clippings, government reports, and articles and books sent to him by friends and advisers, Reagan wrote his five-minute commentaries with a black-ink felt pen on a yellow legal pad. Academic Kiron K. Skinner discovered 670 handwritten manuscripts in the Reagan Presidential Library twenty years later and, along with Hoover fellows Martin and Annelise Anderson, published a broad sampling of them in 2001. Surveying the voluminous research and writing required to produce the commentaries, the editors described Reagan as "a one-man think tank."[26]

The broadcasts outlined Reagan's conservative vision for America—a vision of faith and freedom that would restore Americans' confidence in themselves and their country, reignite the nation's engines of economic progress, and initiate a winning policy in the Cold War. The main goal of America's foreign policy, Reagan argued, should be to defeat communism through such measures as a strong military and support of the "captive nations" behind the Iron Curtain. In one commentary, he used language that anticipated his famous 1982 comment to the British Parliament that communism was headed for the ash heap of history. "Communism is neither an economic or a political system," he said, "it is a form of insanity—a temporary aberration which will one day disappear from the earth because it is contrary to human nature." In another broadcast, Reagan said that "nothing proves the failure of Marxism more than the Soviet Union's inability to produce weapons for its military ambitions and at the same time provide for their peoples every day." His conclusion: "Maybe there is an answer. We simply do what's morally right. Stop doing business with them. Let their system collapse."[27]

In the area of domestic and economic policy, Reagan stressed the importance of tax cuts and less government regulation. In June 1977, he talked about the need for income tax indexing—a key ingredient of his 1981 Economic Recovery Tax Act. On several occasions, he criticized the weaknesses of the Social Security system and urged the creation of personal savings accounts that could "double the return promised by Social Security."[28]

Nor did he neglect social issues. Regarding abortion, he said, "My answer as to what kind of abortion bill I could sign was one that recognized an abortion is the taking of a human life." He criticized the Supreme Court's decision to "expel" God from our public schools. "Christmas can be celebrated in the school room with pine trees, tinsel, and reindeers," he noted ironically, "but there must be no mention of the man whose birthday is celebrated. One wonders how a teacher would answer if a student asked why it was called Christmas."[29]

When a Fayetteville, Tennessee, listener wrote Reagan to complain that all he did was criticize the government and to suggest that he be taken off the air, he responded with a succinct explanation of the proper role of government and the responsibilities of the electorate. "I believe in this system and don't believe it has ever failed us. We have failed it many times. When a national poll reveals that only 46 percent of the people can name their U.S. congressman . . . we are not practicing government by the people." He quoted Lincoln that it was "possible to be loyal to government and still be critical of those in power." He emphasized that "you will never hear me assail our system or the Constitution." What he wanted, he summed up, "is the same freedom for today's young people that I knew when I was growing up."[30]

Reagan estimated in October 1978 that through his daily radio broadcasts and biweekly newspaper columns he was in touch with twenty million Americans each week—an impressive potential electoral base for a presidential candidate. At last the signal was given, and in early March 1979, Senator Paul Laxalt announced the formation of the Reagan for President Committee. Three years earlier, Laxalt had been a lonely Washington voice for Reagan—one of only two members of Congress to support the former California governor. This time, he was joined by a dozen senators and congressmen and over 365 prominent Republicans as founding members of the exploratory committee. Included were several former Ford administration officials like Treasury Secretary William Simon and Health, Education and Welfare Secretary Caspar Weinberger.

It was a good time for a conservative to run for president. By the end of 1979, after three years of the inept Carter presidency, the inflation rate stood at 13.3 percent—the highest since the Korean War and nearly double the 7.2 percent Carter had inherited from Ford. Unemployment stood at 8 percent—Carter had promised as a candidate in 1976 that he would reduce it to 4 percent. Confronted by mounting economic woes, an obdurate Carter refused to blame himself or his administration's maladroit decisions. Instead, he faulted the American people who, he said, were deep in the throes of a "crisis of confidence."[31] He did not mention that they were also being strangled by "stagflation"—double-digit inflation coupled with zero economic growth.

Things were even worse abroad. The pro-West Shah of Iran had been ousted, Marxist regimes were established in Angola and Mozambique, the pro-Castro Sandinistas took control of Nicaragua, and the Soviets invaded Afghanistan. Casting about for an explanation of communism's global aggression, Andrew Young, Carter's ambassador to the United Nations, went Orwellian, asserting that the thirty thousand Cuban troops in Angola brought "a certain stability and order to the country."[32]

Reagan and his campaign team knew that their first and most important task was to win the New Hampshire primary—the narrow loss to Ford in 1976 still rankled. And to do that, the candidate would have to overcome the opinion held by some voters and many journalists that he was too old, too conservative, and not smart enough to be president. Reagan supporters readily admitted that if elected, their candidate would be at sixty-nine the oldest man ever to assume the presidency. But they reminded everyone that the post–World War II world had been dominated by old lions like Winston Churchill, Charles de Gaulle, Konrad Adenauer, and Dwight Eisenhower, all of whom were older than Reagan when in office. Asked about his age, Reagan characteristically replied with humor. "You know, I was in the Orient last year," he told one audience. "They thought I was too young."[33] He said he had watched a rerun of *Knute Rockne—All American* and that it was like "seeing a younger son I never knew I had." He compared himself to Giuseppe Verdi, who composed the opera *Falstaff* when he was eighty, and to Antonius Stradivarius, who made his best violins after he turned sixty.[34]

Reagan was prepared to campaign from coast to coast to demonstrate his stamina, and to prove he could do it, he underwent in October 1979 a head-to-toe physical examination, and received a glowing report. He was six feet one inch tall and weighed 185 pounds, almost the same as in his college football days. His blood pressure was 130/80 following a treadmill stress test. He did not take any medication aside from shots for a chronic allergy. He had hearing loss in both ears from being exposed to gunfire in a 1930s film, but did not, as yet, require a hearing aid. (He did start wearing a device early in his first term.) He exercised every day, even when on the road. And he did all the tough muscle-stretching chores at Rancho del Cielo. He had helped remodel the simple two-bedroom Spanish-style home in which he and Nancy spent many of their weekends and vacations. He liked to point out that he had built a fence around their home out of old telephone poles and had constructed a rock patio—not bad for an "old" man who looked at least a decade younger than his sixty-eight years.

As for being too conservative, a Harris poll revealed that the majority of Americans liked Ronald Reagan's right-of-center philosophy. More than half disagreed that he was "too conservative," and nearly 60 percent felt that he "has a highly attractive personality and would inspire confidence as president." A solid majority also agreed that Reagan "is right to want to get government out of business so that free enterprise can operate freely."[35] And he enjoyed a national recognition among Republicans that was equaled only by former president Gerald Ford. An August 1977 Gallup poll found that Reagan was known by nine out of ten Americans and was their first choice as the next Republican presidential nominee.[36]

In announcing his candidacy on November 13, 1979, over a special network of television stations that reached an estimated 79 percent of the electorate, Reagan pledged a 30 percent tax cut along the lines of the bill introduced by Representative Jack Kemp of New York and Senator William Roth of Delaware; an orderly transfer of federal programs to the state and local levels along with the funds to pay for them (no $90 billion gaffe this time); a revitalized energy program based on increased production of oil, natural gas, and coal through deregulation; the development of a long-range diplomatic and military strategy to meet the challenge of the Soviet Union; and a North American economic accord among the United States, Canada, and Mexico.

He concluded with words familiar to Reagan watchers but more appealing than ever before to a people wondering whether their best days were behind them:

A troubled and afflicted mankind looks to us, pleading for us to keep our rendezvous with destiny; that we will uphold the principles of self-reliance, self-discipline, morality, and—above all—responsible liberty for every individual; that we will become that shining city on a hill.

I believe that you and I together can keep this rendezvous with destiny.[37]

Despite formidable competition, Reagan was the front-runner, routinely receiving 40 to 50 percent in Republican polls. Senate Republican leader Howard Baker of Tennessee had been campaigning hard but still trailed far behind. Former Treasury secretary John Connally of Texas was not catching on with Republicans, who viewed the one-time Democratic governor as something of a turncoat. Senator Bob Dole, the 1976 vice presidential nominee, was poorly organized and often abrasive on the stump. Illinois representative Phil Crane's slim chances depended on Reagan's faltering. Representative John Anderson of Illinois was too liberal for three-fourths of the party he wanted to lead. George Herbert Walker Bush, the man with the golden resume, had put together a good campaign organization but still nestled near the bottom of the challengers with about 3 percent; he had not won an election since 1968 when he was reelected to the Congress from Houston.

The first test came on January 21, 1980, with the Iowa precinct caucuses. Reagan hardly campaigned in the state (forty-one hours in all), even declining to participate in a Des Moines debate two weeks before the caucus vote. He was following the "Rose Garden" strategy carefully plotted by campaign manager John Sears, once again running things despite the wrenching 1976 loss. "It wouldn't do any good to have him going to coffees and shaking hands like the others," explained Sears haughtily. "People will get the idea he's an ordinary man, like the rest of us."[38] In the final seven weeks of 1979 and the first three of 1980, wrote Lou Cannon, Reagan was "an airborne celebrity candidate, soaring above the earthbound struggles of mortal contenders for the Republican nomination."[39]

But Iowa Republicans were not interested in having a demi-god in the White House and, like most voters, wanted to feel wanted. Thousands of them turned out for Bush, who, after campaigning thirty-one grueling days in snow-bound Iowa, boasted he had spent more days in Iowa than Reagan had hours. Bush narrowly defeated Reagan, 33 percent to 30 percent, and was immediately dubbed the front-runner. Sears pointed out, correctly, that his candidate had done extremely well for someone who had hardly campaigned. However, many political analysts, recalling Reagan's 1976 stumbles in New Hampshire and Florida, wondered aloud whether Reagan, for all his star power, was capable of winning a presidential nomination. Lyn Nofziger, who had been forced out of the campaign by Sears, commented: "If you're going to follow a Rose Garden strategy, you better be sure you have a Rose Garden."[40]

Conscious that everything now depended on his capturing New Hampshire, a determined Reagan abandoned Sears's imperial strategy and doubled his schedule of speeches, barnstorming all over the Granite State in a bus for almost three weeks. "I have practically taken up residence [here] as you suggested," he wrote me. (I was one of many who had made the suggestion). "I don't mind telling you I'm running scared."[41] Gerald Carmen, the former chairman of the state Republican Party, built a network of Reagan volunteers, including members of single-issue groups like right-to-life and antigun control, and directed it from a crowded, chaotic, phones-ringing-every-second office in downtown Manchester. Liberal columnist Mark Shields, contrasting Carmen's working-class background with the upscale past of Bush manager Susan McLane, suggested that the race was "between Schlitz and sherry, between citizenship papers and collected papers, between night school and graduate school."[42] Asked to spell out the differences between himself and Bush, Reagan said that Bush favored a liberalized abortion law, the Equal Rights Amendment, and a guaranteed-income welfare plan, all of which he opposed.

An eager Reagan agreed to debate not once but twice in New Hampshire. After the first debate among all contenders, his polls told him he had won, but he was still only slightly ahead of Bush. The second debate was the turning point in New Hampshire and, indeed, in the entire primary season. It was a telling example of high-stakes politics, with Reagan conducting himself flawlessly and Bush committing a series of blunders.

Reagan had agreed to a one-on-one debate with Bush in Nashua under the sponsorship of the local newspaper, the *Nashua Telegraph*. But the Federal Election Commission ruled that the paper's sponsorship constituted an illegal campaign contribution because it benefited only two candidates. Reagan proposed that he and Bush split the $3,500 cost of the debate. But Bush refused because his campaign was close to its spending limit, so Reagan sent a check for the whole amount. When the other candidates began complaining that they had been excluded, Reagan (at Sears's suggestion) invited all of them to participate.

The night of the debate, Bush strode into the gym alone and seated himself in one of the two chairs on the stage. Reagan then marched onto the stage along with four other candidates. While Reagan sat on the other reserved chair, Baker, Dole, Anderson, and Crane lined up behind him. People in the audience began shouting, "Get them chairs, get them chairs!"

Bush refused to acknowledge the four standing men, all prominent fellow Republicans vying for the presidency. When Reagan began trying to explain the situation, Jon Breen, the debate moderator and *Telegraph* editor, shouted, "Will the sound man please turn Mr. Reagan's mike off?" The audience burst into loud boos. A red-faced Reagan seized his microphone and shouted in raw anger, "I'm paying for this microphone, Mr. Green!"[43]

Although Reagan got the moderator's name wrong, his passionate outburst won the cheers of the audience. Sitting in the audience, veteran political reporter David Broder said quietly, "Reagan is winning this primary right now." The image of an aroused and assertive Reagan was featured in every New Hampshire newspaper, television, and radio report for the next forty-eight hours. Meanwhile, a shaken Bush said weakly, "I will play by the rules, and I'm glad to be here."[44] Not appreciating the measure of his miscalculation, Bush flew home to Houston and was pictured jogging in the Texas sun while Reagan slogged through the New Hampshire snow all weekend and right up to primary day. In what had once been regarded as a close contest, Reagan buried Bush by more than 2 to 1, 51 percent to 22 percent, collecting as many votes as his six rivals combined. He also buried his campaign manager John Sears, who made the mistake of often acting as though he were more indispensable to the campaign than Reagan. "I look him in the eye," complained Reagan, "and he looks me in the tie."[45] The new manager was New York lawyer and longtime conservative William Casey (who would become Reagan's controversial CIA director).

The political momentum now shifted sharply. By the end of March, Baker, Connally, and Dole had withdrawn from the Republican nomination race, followed in April by Crane and Anderson. But Anderson, who had not won any of the nine Republican primaries he entered, declared himself to be an "Independent" and announced that a committee would study whether he could get his name on enough state ballots to win the presidency and whether sufficient money could be raised for a national campaign.

Reagan kept beating Bush—in Texas, his home state; in New York, the center of the Eastern liberal establishment; in Michigan, the hub of organized labor; and in Oregon, the most liberal of the Western states. Finally, on May 26 (before California), Bush conceded the 1980 Republican presidential nomination to Ronald Reagan. Bush's decision not to continue was realistic and politic: he was widely mentioned as a possible running mate for Reagan.

When CBS's Mike Wallace asked Reagan in an interview whether it wasn't "arrogant" of him to want to take over the direction of "the greatest superpower in the world," the candidate replied calmly, "I find myself very conscious of the size and difficulty of the undertaking." But bear in mind, he added, that in seeking the office he was not being politically ambitious. An astonished Wallace asked Reagan to explain what he meant. "I'm not on any ego trip or glory ride," Reagan said. "I'm running because I think there is a job to do and I want to do it."[46]

The Dream Ticket

Already energized by the prospect of Reagan's nomination, Republicans meeting in Detroit for the national convention were treated to one of those outbursts of irrationality that, like sudden summer storms, sometimes sweep across mass political meetings. The catalyst was an unexpectedly dynamic speech on opening night by former President Ford, who declared, "This country means too much to me to comfortably park on the park bench. So, when this convention fields the team for Governor Reagan, count me in."[47] Maybe, the delegates began saying to each other, we ought to field a Reagan-Ford team. Top Republicans, conservative, moderate, and liberal, tried to make it happen.

At Reagan's initiative, the two political leaders met and then asked their aides to see if they could arrive at a compromise regarding the shared duties and responsibilities of a future president and a past president. The turning point came, as often happens in our media age, over national television. Over CBS, Ford revealed he was seriously considering the vice presidency. Walter Cronkite asked Ford directly, "It's got to be something like a co-presidency?" Although "copresidency" was not his word, Ford did not reject it, replying, "That's something Governor Reagan really ought to consider."[48] Watching in his hotel, Reagan was dismayed: No one had suggested there ought to be two presidents in the White House. While their aides continued to struggle with language, like diplomats over a final communiqué, Ford and Reagan separately decided at almost the same moment that it wouldn't work. Meeting in Reagan's suite, the once and future presidents talked for only ten minutes, but with no tension or bitterness, about the collapse of the "dream ticket." "He was a gentleman," Reagan said afterward about Ford. "I feel we're friends now."[49]

Eager to assert his command of the convention and to prevent the TV networks from rumor-mongering throughout the night and into the morning, Reagan telephoned a surprised George Bush, who thought along with most of America that Reagan-Ford was a done deal. "I plan to go over to the convention," revealed Reagan, "and tell them you are my first choice for the nomination." An elated Bush responded, "I can campaign enthusiastically for your election and your platform."[50]

Reagan's pursuit of Ford is illustrative of his pragmatism, inventiveness, and quick reflexes. To implement his conservative ideas, he had to get elected, and if Jerry Ford would help him achieve that end, he was willing to run with someone he once criticized for allowing America to become "dangerously weak." It did not bother him that picking a former president as his running mate was unprecedented: he was not bound to the past, only respectful of it. When the proposed merger collapsed, he acted swiftly to line up a replacement almost as acceptable to all parts of the Republican Party.

Reagan's acceptance address (drafted by longtime aide Peter Hannaford) sought to bind together all the elements of the GOP, while also reaching out to Independents and disillusioned Democrats. It articulated the traditional sources of American thought from the Mayflower Compact to the founding fathers to Lincoln's Gettysburg Address, and ended with a quotation from Franklin D. Roosevelt attacking excessive government spending, followed by a silent moment of prayer for the hostages in Iran. Its central theme was summed up in five words—"family, work, neighborhood, peace, freedom"—that would serve as guideposts for his administration. Although many in the national news media did not understand the emphasis on FDR, Reagan was reaching out to Americans, especially Democrats, who had lost confidence in President Carter and remembered the days when the White House was "the source of effective national leadership." Reagan was confident most Americans wanted that kind of leadership again.[51]

Although all the national polls placed Reagan well ahead of Carter right after the Republican convention, the president got a sizable bump from the Democratic convention and some rhetorical mistakes in August by Reagan, such as suggesting—at a national rally of evangelical Christians—that "creationism" ought to be taught in the schools as an alternative to Darwin's theory of evolution. By Labor Day, the two candidates were about even. But, as Lou Cannon neatly put it, Carter was dogged by the captivity of hostages he could not free, an economy he could not improve, and an opponent he could not shake.[52]

A grimly determined Carter never stopped trying. He rolled out the usual anticonservative arsenal of charges, portraying Reagan as a right-wing extremist opposed to peace, arms control, and working people—a man who would divide the country. The president played the race card early and often, accusing Reagan of injecting hatred and racism into the campaign by using code words like "states' rights." Appearing at Martin Luther King Jr.'s church in Atlanta, Georgia, Carter grinned and shook the hand of U.S. Representative Parren Mitchell of Maryland, who had just said of Reagan, "I'm going to talk about a man . . . who seeks the presidency of the United States with the endorsement of the Ku Klux Klan."[53] It did not matter to Mitchell or Carter, apparently, that Reagan had immediately repudiated the Klan's endorsement.

Every candidate needs someone whom he respects and who will not hesitate to tell him the truth, no matter how discomforting, about the way the campaign is going. Reagan drafted blunt, irreverent, shrewd Stu Spencer, who had managed his first campaign back in 1966. Reagan set about courting the blue-collar, ethnic Catholic vote, concentrating on Carter's sorry economic record, and endeavoring to reassure the voters he could handle the weighty duties of the presidency. When the president refused to participate in a three-way debate with Reagan and John Anderson, Reagan readily agreed to appear with his Independent opponent. The 55 million Americans who watched the Reagan-Anderson debate on September 21 were treated to an impressive political demonstration. The answers pointed up the sharp differences between the two candidates, with Reagan urging smaller government and less spending and Anderson proposing billion-dollar government solutions for the problems of energy and the inner city. Reagan repeated his call for a 10 percent tax cut for each of the next three years, noting that his proposal "has been called inflationary by my opponent, by the man who isn't here tonight."[54]

Although one poll reported that viewers believed Anderson had "outplayed" Reagan, the results of a *New York Times*/CBS poll suggested that Reagan was the true beneficiary because a greater number of people believed that the former governor understood the complicated problems facing a president, had a clear position on the issues, offered a clear vision of where he wanted to lead the country, and would exercise good judgment under pressure. The poll reported that Reagan now led Carter by five points.

Reagan was now campaigning smoothly, presenting specialized messages to key constituencies in the communities he visited. In Miami, he denounced Fidel Castro and promised that America would remain a refuge for those fleeing tyranny. In Springfield, Missouri, he criticized Carter for hesitating to declare the state a disaster area following a severe drought. In Tyler, Texas, he charged that Carter was afraid to debate energy policy with him. And in Grand Junction, Colorado, he declared that Westerners knew how to manage their water resources better than the federal bureaucracy did. The content of his speeches was traditional Republican—cut taxes, limit government—but his style was traditional Democrat, with constant references to family, neighborhood, work, and peace.

Responding to the negative polls and reports from the field, Carter became increasingly strident, telling a Chicago audience, for example, that it would be "a catastrophe" if Reagan were elected. You will determine, he said, his voice rising and almost breaking, "whether or not this America will be unified or, if I lose this election, whether Americans might be separated, black from white, Jew from Christian, North from South, rural from urban." Asked to comment, Reagan said he was "saddened" by the remarks and that Carter owed, not him, but the country an apology.[55]

With two weeks left in the campaign, Reagan held a narrow lead of about seven points in the popular vote and a comfortable margin in the electoral vote. But the Reagan organization was concerned about one issue over which it had no control: the fifty-three American hostages in Iran. If they were freed at the eleventh hour, how would the public react? Would the American people be caught up in the euphoria of the moment and reelect Carter? Or would they dismiss the release as October politics and vote their pocketbooks? Reagan and most of his advisers—with pollster Richard Wirthlin and political adviser William Timmons dissenting—concluded they could not afford to sit on a safe but slim lead and played their last card—a televised debate with Jimmy Carter. They were confident that Reagan could more than hold his own.

On Tuesday, October 28, one week before election day, the two candidates stood behind specially constructed rostrums on the stage of Cleveland's Music Hall for their one and only debate of the 1980 presidential campaign. Their audience was an estimated 105 million Americans.

Both men wore dark suits and muted ties. The similarities ended there. Carter was tight-lipped and stood rigid, rarely looking at his opponent. He immediately went on the attack and stayed there for ninety minutes, constantly describing his opponent's ideas and positions as "dangerous," "disturbing," and "radical."[56]

Reagan was calm, cool, smiling. He spent much of his time patiently explaining where Carter had misquoted or misrepresented him, much like a professor gently pointing out the errors of an overzealous student. The climax of the debate—and the effective end of the campaign—came when Carter tried to link Reagan with the idea of making social security voluntary and argued that Reagan had opposed Medicare. (Reagan had in fact supported an alternate sponsored by the American Medical Association.) That familiar crooked grin appeared on Reagan's face, and with a rueful shake of his head, he looked at Carter and said, "There you go again."[57] The Carter campaign of fear collapsed in an instant.

Reagan sealed Carter's defeat and his victory with his closing remarks when he looked straight into the camera and quietly asked the viewer:

> Are you better off than you were four years ago? Is it easier for you to go and buy things in the stores than it was four years ago? Is America as respected throughout the world as it was? Do you feel our security is as safe, that we're as strong as we were four years ago?[58]

An Associated Press poll found that 46 percent of those watching thought Reagan did the better job, with 34 percent saying Carter did. A CBS survey revealed Reagan the winner over Carter by 44 percent to 36 percent. The same survey showed that undecided voters were moving toward Reagan by a two-to-one margin.[59] And then on Sunday, November 2, forty-eight hours before election day, the Iranian parliament announced its terms for freeing the hostages. Carter dramatically interrupted his campaigning to fly to Washington to confer with his top security advisers. He went on national television Sunday afternoon to say that the conditions "appear to offer a positive basis" for an acceptable agreement.[60] But the October surprise on which the Carter campaign had been depending turned out to be a November insult—Iran made demands that would have required extended negotiations. There was no triumphal return of the hostages before the voters went to the polls.

On the eve of the election, when a reporter asked Reagan what he thought other Americans saw in him, he replied, "Would you laugh if I told you that I think, maybe, they see themselves and that I'm one of them?" He added, in an unusually revealing comment, "I've never been able to detach myself or think that I, somehow, am apart from them."[61]

Although most of the national polls said it would be a close election, Reagan won by an electoral landslide and more than 8 million popular votes. He carried forty-four states (the same number as Lyndon Johnson in his 1964 runaway victory over conservative Barry Goldwater) with a total of 489 electoral votes. His 43.9 million votes were the second largest total on record, behind only Richard Nixon's 47.2 million in 1972. His political coattails helped the GOP to pick up twelve seats in the Senate, giving it majority control for the first time in a quarter of a century. In the House, Republicans registered a gain of 33 seats, almost all of them conservatives.

Former Democratic presidential candidate George McGovern said flatly that the voters had "abandoned American liberalism." In an editorial titled, "Tidal Wave," the *Washington Post* acknowledged that 1980 was not an ordinary election year: "Nothing of that size and force and sweep could have been created over a weekend or even a week or two by the assorted mullahs and miseries of our times." Pollster Louis Harris concluded that Reagan had won "his stunning victory" because conservatives of all varieties, particularly the Moral Majority, "gave him such massive support."[62]

Reagan won because he dominated the five key elements of every political campaign—money, organization, the candidates, issues, and the media. And he won because he was a man with an idea whose time had come. The idea was that government had grown too big and should be reduced, and America's military had grown too weak and ought to be strengthened. The result, Reagan argued, would be peace and prosperity. The American people liked the sound of that and elected him president.

Nevertheless, as Reagan prepared to occupy the highest office in the land at a time of foreign as well as domestic crisis, even sympathetic conservatives like author Richard Whalen asked openly: Had political success come so easily for Reagan that he would be unprepared for the inevitable failures of the presidency? Had his long experience in addressing mostly friendly audiences "bred a streak of self-indulgence" that might crack in the face of hostile adversaries? As president, would he continue to "shoot from the lip" as he sometimes had as a candidate and even as governor? (Once, while discussing California's magnificent redwoods, he said, "A tree is a tree—how many more do you need to look at?"). Was he a thinking conservative or merely a script-reader?[63]

CHAPTER 6

Golden Years

The new president and his top advisers were well aware they had to act, and swiftly. In presidential politics, as in the one-hundred-yard dash, a quick start is everything.

Richard Wirthlin, the president's pollster and a senior adviser, had developed "a strategic outline of initial actions" to be taken during the administration's first 180 days—from the inauguration to early August, when Congress usually recessed for a summer vacation. The outline, based on Reagan's philosophy and not political expediency, drew in large part on an address that Reagan had delivered in September 1980 before the International Business Council of Chicago. Candidate Reagan had proposed strictly controlling the rate of growth of government spending, reducing personal income tax rates, revising government regulations, establishing a stable monetary policy, and following a consistent national economic policy.

Democrats had attacked the Reagan proposal with abandon, and big business mouthpieces like the National Association of Manufacturers had complained because the plan did not cut business taxes enough. But research director Martin Anderson and the other numbers crunchers were confident: they had produced a document (with projections through 1985) showing that Reagan could cut taxes, balance the budget, and increase domestic growth given the right kind of cooperation by Congress. The *Wall Street Journal* agreed, commenting that Reagan had "spelled out a prudent, gradual, responsible reordering of economic priorities."[1]

The first and most decisive step was tax reform. The top marginal rate on individual income was 70 percent, and Reagan, who had read extensively in the field since the 1950s and had himself paid a 91 percent personal income tax in the 1940s, insisted that if you reduced tax rates and allowed people to spend or save more of what they earned, "they'll be more industrious, they'll have more incentive to work hard, and money they earn will add fuel to the great economic machine that energizes our national progress." Some economists called this approach "supply-side economics." "I call it common sense," Reagan said.[2]

As early as 1964 in his seminal television speech for Barry Goldwater, Reagan had sharply criticized the high taxes and large subsidies demanded by America's welfare state and warned, "No nation in history has ever survived a tax burden that reached one-third of its national income." As governor of California, he had striven to reduce taxes, even sponsoring a tax limitation amendment to the state constitution. Reagan was a supply-sider, wrote Edwin Meese III, his longtime colleague, "long before the term was invented."[3]

It took fireside chats with the American people, deals with moderate "boll-weevil" Democrats in the House of Representatives, pep talks with exhausted aides, and recovery from an attempted assassination, but on August 17, 1981, President Reagan signed the Economic Recovery Tax Act (ERTA) into law. *Newsweek* called it a "second New Deal potentially as profound in its import as the first was a half century ago."[4] The measure cut *all* income tax rates by 25 percent, with a 5 percent cut coming that October, the next 10 percent in July 1982, and the final 10 percent in July 1983. It reduced the top income tax rate from 70 percent to 50 percent, indexed tax rates to offset the impact of inflation, and increased the tax exemption on estates and gifts. Although the act's impact was not immediate, it was measurable, starting in the fall of 1982.

Economic growth over the next ninety-two months (through 1990) was the longest uninterrupted economic expansion in peacetime in the twentieth century. It was bested only by the Kennedy-Johnson years of 1961 to 1969 when we were at war in Vietnam. Some 17 million new jobs were created during 1981 to 1989. By the end of 1987, America was producing about seven and one-half times more every year than it produced in John Kennedy's last year as president. Unemployment by the end of 1988 was 5.5 percent of the labor force, having decreased steadily from its peak of 9.7 percent in the depths of the 1981–1982 recession. Stock market averages more than doubled during the Reagan years.[5]

In the period between mid-1981 and late 1982 when the tax cuts had not yet kicked in and the anxiety of his staff and congressional Republicans was rising, Reagan's admonition was always the same: stay the course. As he had from his days as governor of California, he drew encouragement from his correspondence with old friends and new acquaintances. He was touched by the story of a young black mother of four children who was separated from her husband and on welfare. But she "managed to get herself a high school diploma, and now is setting out to get off welfare and be self-sufficient." His trust in America had been renewed by her courage and faith.[6]

The economic expansion was felt everywhere, as conservative economists and Reagan himself had predicted, including in government income. Total federal revenues in 1981 were $618 billion; seven years later, they were $909.3 billion. And as the president had promised the military benefited handsomely from the economic growth. In President Carter's last budget, America spent just under $160 billion on national defense. In 1988, the Reagan administration spent $304 billion, including more than twice as much on military hardware. During Reagan's eight years in office, he expended $1.72 trillion on national defense, an awesome amount by anyone's standards.

Reagan did not hesitate to go against the grain, as when, in one of his first acts as president, he ended price controls on petroleum. The *New York Times* quickly dismissed the president's faith in the free market and predicted his action would produce "declining domestic oil production" and skyrocketing gasoline prices. Within four months, the price of gasoline fell by more than sixty cents a gallon, but there was no apology from the *Times*.[7]

Although Reagan promised deep cuts in domestic spending, that did not happen. Overall welfare spending increased during the Reagan presidency, primarily because Reagan could not overcome, even with vetoes and the bully pulpit of the White House, the spending impulses of Congress, which signed the checks. Throughout his two terms, he was confronted by Democrats still enthralled by the New Deal as well as Republicans (especially in the Senate) still mesmerized by its political appeal. Reagan was not discouraged—he understood he would have to cut carefully, $1 billion at a time. He could not just pull the plug on the federal government. Over the past fifty years, since the birth of the New Deal, millions of people had become dependent on government.

Many remember Reagan saying in his inaugural address that "government is not the solution to our problems; government is the problem." But the new president also said:

It is not my intention to do away with government. It is rather to make it work—work with us, not over us; to stand by our side, not ride on our back. Government can and must provide opportunity, not smother it; foster productivity, not stifle it.[8]

Here was no radical libertarian with a copy of *Atlas Shrugged* on his desk but a traditional conservative guided by the prudential reasoning of *The Federalist*. Reagan was, in fact, a modern federalist, echoing James Madison's call for a balance between the authority of the national and state governments. He also shared Madison's concern about "the abridgement of the freedom of the people" by the "gradual and silent encroachment of those in power." As Reagan later said in his 1990 autobiography, "We had strayed a great distance from our founding fathers' vision of America."[9]

He was determined to recapture that lost vision. In his inaugural, he promised to begin by seeking "to curb the size and influence of the federal establishment." Revealing his pragmatism, his immediate target was the welfare excesses of Lyndon B. Johnson, not the long-established social programs of Franklin D. Roosevelt. As he wrote in his diary, "The press is trying to paint me as trying to undo the New Deal. I'm trying to undo the Great Society."[10]

It was a slow process, made more difficult by a Democratic House of Representatives led by the fiercely partisan Speaker Tip O'Neill from Massachusetts. Reagan was obliged to allow federal spending for welfare—in such areas as education and training, social services, medicine, food, and housing—to rise sharply; expenditures almost doubled from $106.1 billion (in real or nominal dollars) in 1980 to $173 billion in 1988. Conservative critics like the Heritage Foundation's Stuart Butler did not hide their disappointment. Six years into the Reagan presidency, Butler wrote that "the basic structure of the Great Society is still firmly intact. . . . Virtually no program has been eliminated."[11]

But Reagan did reduce federal outlays in some welfare areas such as regional development, commerce, and housing credit from $63 billion in 1980 to just over $49 billion in 1987, a decrease of about 22 percent. And the size of the federal civilian workforce declined by about 5 percent, much of it traceable to conservatives like Gerald Carmen of the General Services Administration, Raymond Donovan of the Department of Labor, and the

Office of Personnel Management's Donald Devine, described by the *Washington Post* as "Reagan's terrible swift sword of the civil service."[12]

Five principles guided the Reagan welfare cuts, drawn from the California experience: The growth of government should be curbed; federal benefits should be focused primarily on the poor; benefits should be contingent on an individual's effort to leave welfare; decisions on social programs should be returned to the states and localities; and programs that do not work should be eliminated. At the heart of these principles was a simple proposition: Entitlements as the "underlying principle of American social policy" should be replaced by "benefits contingent on responsible behavior."[13]

Reagan's personal feelings about Social Security had not changed since his 1964 televised address for Barry Goldwater, when he had suggested the introduction of "voluntary features [into the system] that would permit a citizen to do better on his own" if he wanted to.[14] But he had come to accept, reluctantly, that social security was an issue that Republicans could not touch without getting badly burned. Two months into his presidency, the White House was given a congressional initiative that would have sharply slowed the growth of social security and reduced the budget deficit. The device was to institute a freeze or even a severe reduction in automatic cost-of-living allowances, which had increased social security payments so much that the program now accounted for 21 percent of the total budget.

Reagan was tempted, but as he told Senator Pete Domenici of New Mexico, the author of the amendment and chairman of the Senate Budget Committee, "I made a commitment during the campaign not to cut Social Security, and . . . I don't want to go back on my word."[15] Other senators, including conservatives John Tower of Texas and William Armstrong of Colorado, endorsed Domenici's approach, but Reagan would not be moved. He had given his word, publicly, and that was that.

There is no denying that American indebtedness increased significantly during the Reagan years. The Reagan administration borrowed $1 for every $5 it spent, increasing the national debt by $1.61 trillion through 1988. But it did not have to worry about where to get the money. America was such a good credit risk, wrote one observer, that people around the world "pressed money on us, and we obliged, borrowing easily, quickly, and almost guiltlessly."[16] But Reagan did feel guilty about the accumulated debt—as much as anyone with his unassailable optimism could feel guilty. He admitted that his failures to cut federal spending absolutely and to balance the federal budget were his "biggest disappointments" as president.[17] But as he said repeatedly, publicly and privately, if it came to a choice between "balancing the budget or rebuilding our defenses, I'd come down on the side of the latter."[18]

By the end of the Reagan era, however, economist Stephen Moore emphasized, the federal deficit as a share of gross domestic product (GDP) was falling, and rapidly—from 6.3 percent in 1983 to 2.9 percent in 1989. As Reagan left office, the Congressional Budget Office projected that "deficits were on a path to fall to about 1 percent of GDP" by 1993 without any action by future presidents.[19]

Reagan never ignored the deficit—he just had more important things on his mind. "I did not come here to balance the budget," he said in 1981, certainly "not at the expense of my tax-cutting program and my defense program."[20] Still, every budget he submitted to Congress outlined spending reductions that would have reduced the cumulative deficit during the 1980s by several hundred billion dollars. But Congress nullified this possibility with a succession of "continuing resolutions" that enabled the government to keep operating and spending at the same level.

Still the persistent deficits sobered the usually freewheeling Congress, which for the first time in the postwar era began to impose limits on the growth of government. Of all the measures we know, Nobel economist Milton Friedman wrote, "the deficit has been the only effective restraint on congressional spending."[21]

President Reagan devoted most of his time in the spring and early summer of 1981 (after he had recovered from the March 30 shooting by would-be assassin John Hinckley) building a consensus for his economic recovery program. *Time*'s Lawrence Barrett described the president's strategy as initial "seduction" followed by a "blitzkrieg."[22] Reagan began by showing the Washington establishment that he was not a dangerous man or a "political freak." He had drinks with Speaker Tip O'Neill, a meeting with Senator Edward Kennedy, a chat with *Washington Post* publisher Katharine Graham. Quite a charmer, they agreed, but no real threat to the way Washington works.

O'Neill was so deceived that he condescendingly offered some advice to the new fellow in town. "You were governor of a state," he told Reagan, "but a governor plays in the minor leagues. Now you're in the big leagues." Reagan was more amused than offended, secure in his objectives and his tactics. He personally lobbied hundreds of Congressmen and opinion-makers (including CBS's Walter Cronkite). He delivered a televised appeal to the public—in prime time—asking them to let their representatives know they supported the president's economic program. The following day congressional offices were flooded with telephone calls and telegrams. He got almost everything he wanted in negotiations with the Democratic leadership who never comprehended how skillfully they were being handled. They would make compromises, biographer Dinesh D'Souza points out, and expect Reagan to accept them, but he wouldn't. When they would give a little more, Reagan would say: "I cannot bring myself to do this." And then when the Democrats's patience was finally exhausted and they had given as much as they could, Reagan would prevail on them to concede just one more thing, and then suddenly he would sign. An exasperated O'Neill protested that Reagan's style of bargaining verged on "blackmail," causing Reagan, who had honed his bargaining skills during his years as president of the Screen Actors Guild, to respond with an injured expression.[23]

Eight months after the veteran politician O'Neill welcomed the rookie president to the big leagues, the House of Representatives passed Reagan's economic recovery plan, 238-195, with the cross-over help of forty-eight Democrats who did not mind going against their Speaker when it was in the best interests of their constituents. Reagan called Congress's passage of ERTA "the greatest political victory in half a century." Jubilant conservatives hailed it as a "new economic beginning." The *Washington Post*'s David Broder proclaimed Reagan's tax victory as "one of the most remarkable demonstrations of presidential leadership in modern history."[24] The $162 billion tax cut dwarfed any previous one in the postwar period; President Ford's $22.8 billion reduction in 1975 was a distant second.

Furthermore, the cuts in personal income taxes had a permanency unlike that of any previous tax bill because of the indexing provision. In the past, individuals were pushed into higher tax brackets whenever their income rose along with inflation. ERTA did away with "bracket creep" and prevented cynical politicians from "solving" fiscal deficits by waiting for inflation to increase revenues each year. From now on, Congress had to pass and the president had to sign any tax increase out in the open. How to collect government revenues, said analysts Paul Peterson and Mark Rom, became "the dominating political issue of the 1980s."[25]

The Attempted Assassination

There are several reasons for Ronald Reagan's political success in his first year and indeed throughout his eight years in the White House, including his ability to focus on the important and not the peripheral, the timeliness of his ideas, and his unmatched powers of persuasion. But undergirding his presidency in the minds of most Americans was the example of his courage, humor, and forgiveness following the attempted assassination by John Hinckley on March 30, 1981, the seventieth day of his presidency.

Before and after surgery, Reagan poured forth a stream of humorous comments intended to reassure family, colleagues, and the American people that the Gipper was going to be all right. When a fearful Nancy arrived at the hospital, he greeted her, "Honey, I forgot to duck." She was taken back at how pale her husband was; he would in fact lose more than half of his blood supply because of his bullet wound. On the operating table, he looked up at the green-gowned surgeons surrounding him and quipped, "Please tell me you're Republicans." Responded a doctor, "Mr. President, today everyone's a Republican."[26]

The operation began at 3:30 P.M. about one hour after Reagan had been shot. Dr. Benjamin Aaron, the hospital's chief surgeon, concluded that the flattened bullet (which ricocheted off the presidential limousine before it hit the president) had entered the left side of the chest like a disc, sideways, and had then spun through the lung like a turning ball. "When I found it," Aaron said, "it was about an inch from the heart and aorta, right against the heart's surface, almost. I think there was some kind of Divine Providence or something riding with that bullet. Because it still had a lot of zing and one can only conjecture how much worse things might have been."[27]

It took Aaron over an hour to locate and remove the bullet ("I have never in my life seen a chest like that on a man his age"), following which the bleeding soon stopped. Regaining consciousness at 7:30 P.M., Reagan began writing out jokes on pieces of paper because his nose and throat were filled with tubes. "I am . . . alive, aren't I?" "I'd like to do this scene again— starting at the hotel." (Referring to the Washington Hilton, outside of which he had been shot.) And: "Winston Churchill said that there is no more exhilarating feeling than being shot at without result."[28]

Reagan's recovery from the bullet wound was so quick that he met with Ed Meese, James Baker, and Micheal Deaver the following morning, March 31.

"I should have known I wasn't going to avoid a staff meeting," he remarked, smiling, and signed a bill to show he was still in charge. But four nights after the operation, Reagan developed a high fever caused by a stubborn staph infection that did not recede for nearly a week. The public was not informed of the president's second serious illness. Nevertheless, on April 11, just eleven days after Hinckley's attack, a smiling Reagan, thinner by ten pounds, walked out of George Washington Hospital on Nancy's arm (with daughter Patti on the other side) while nurses clapped and cried. The entire White House staff was waiting for him in the Rose Garden when he arrived home. On his first evening back in the White House, he wrote in his diary, "Whatever happens now I owe my life to God and will try to serve him in every way I can."[29] A few weeks later, the president met in the White House with New York's Terence Cardinal Cooke, who said of the attempted assassination and Reagan's speedy recovery, "The hand of God was upon you." "I know," replied Reagan. "I have decided that whatever time I have left is for Him."[30]

Commentators, liberal and conservative alike, lauded Reagan. "The president's imperishable example of grace under pressure," wrote columnist George Will, "gave the nation a tonic it needed." "Everybody knows," wrote the New York Times's James Reston, "that people seldom act at the margin between life and death with such light-hearted valor as they do in the movies. Yet Ronald Reagan did." "To survive danger, to walk tall, to laugh in the face of death," wrote columnist James Jackson Kilpatrick, "this is the stuff of which legend is fashioned."[31]

But Reagan himself preferred to make light of his courage. In late 1981, I visited the White House to present to the president a revised and updated edition of my 1967 biography. In order to promote sales and with a fine disregard for good taste, the publisher had put a bright yellow banner across the cover, proclaiming "Complete through the Assassination Attempt." As President Reagan and I stood chatting in the Oval Office while a photographer snapped pictures, he looked down at the cover and then up at me. "Well, Lee," he said with a crooked smile, "I'm sorry I messed up your ending."[32]

Polls revealed widespread public admiration for Reagan and his presidency. One survey reported 73 percent approval of his performance as president with only 16 percent disapproval. By 72 percent to 23 percent, the public rejected the idea that the president should isolate himself for safety's sake. So did Reagan, determined now more than ever to lead a political reformation to recast the role of government and to end the Cold War in the simplest way possible—by winning it.

People Are Policy

There was a constant struggle throughout the Reagan administration between the Reaganauts, who wanted to transform the government, and the pragmatists, who were content with change at the margin. Between them was the president himself, who sometimes aligned himself with the idealists and sometimes with the pragmatists, seeking a Golden Mean between the two warring camps. He was willing to accept a good deal less than 100 percent if that was all that could be gotten and if the agreement advanced the basic goal of minimizing government and maximizing individual freedom. As he once said of his landmark welfare reforms in California, "If I can get 70 percent of what I want from a legislature controlled by the opposition, I'll take my chances on getting the other thirty when they see how well it works."[33]

Sometimes President Reagan went along with a pragmatist like Chief of Staff James Baker, who persuaded the president to accept the Tax Equity and Fiscal Responsibility Act of 1982 (TEFRA), which turned out to be the great tax increase of 1982—$98 billion over the next three years. Baker assured his boss that Congress would approve three dollars in spending cuts for every dollar of tax increase. To Reagan, TEFRA looked like a "70 percent" deal. But Congress wound up cutting less than twenty-seven cents for every new tax dollar. What had seemed to be an acceptable 70-30 compromise turned out to be a 30-70 surrender. Former White House counselor Ed Meese has described TEFRA as "the greatest domestic error of the Reagan administration," although it did leave untouched the individual tax rate reductions approved the previous year.[34]

The problem was that Reagan believed, as his longtime aide Lyn Nofziger put it, that members of Congress "wouldn't lie to him when he should have known better."[35] As a result of TEFRA, Reagan learned to "trust but verify" whether he was dealing with a Speaker of the House of Representatives or a president of the Soviet Union.

More often the president sided with reformers as when, after a year of hard work, he signed the Tax Reform Act of 1986. In his 1985 State of the Union address, Reagan had signaled his intention "to simplify the tax code so all taxpayers would be treated more fairly."[36] A bipartisan deal was struck between Congressional Democrats and the White House, with Reagan agreeing to close existing tax loopholes if the Democrats would agree to lower marginal rates for individuals and families. Again demonstrating that he would become directly involved in a measure if he felt it necessary, Reagan personally visited Capitol Hill in mid-December 1985 to lobby members of Congress for his tax reform. He later telephoned House Speaker Tip O'Neill to report that he had rounded up more than fifty Republican votes for final passage of the legislation—a requirement O'Neill had set for bringing the Democrat-sponsored bill to the floor.

Describing his plan, a little too enthusiastically, as a Second American Revolution, Reagan said it would make taxes lower, fairer, simpler, and more productive. Indeed, the act lowered the top marginal rate from 50 percent to 33 percent, simplified the number of tax brackets, and increased personal deductions so that an estimated 4.3 million low-income families were removed from the tax rolls. At the same time, a minimum tax was established so that wealthy taxpayers would not escape paying some income tax. And hundreds of special interest provisions, such as deductible "three martini luncheons," were eliminated. Although often overlooked in summaries of the Reagan presidency, the 1986 tax reform initiative was regarded by the president as one of his proudest achievements.

He could also point to other achievements in domestic policy, particularly in his first term: reducing inflation, lowering unemployment, cutting the prime interest rate in half, and producing economic growth of 6 percent in 1983. But his administration was not able to solve all the problems and even failed to tackle some, such as the mounting federal deficit and intrusive federal departments like the Department of Education.

There were several reasons. The federal bureaucracy, protective of its power, began to practice its well-honed delaying tactics. The Democratic opposition, led by the wily Speaker O'Neill, organized more effectively. Pragmatic Reagan aides like James Baker kept resisting bold initiatives. And the complicated budget process (authorization, appropriation, conference committee, etc.) allowed liberal legislators to block White House proposals and whittle away at the president's antispending victories.

Still, the Department of Education, under Terrel H. Bell, appointed the National Commission on Excellence in Education, which produced in 1983 one of the most thoughtful government documents of the Reagan years—*A*

Nation at Risk: The Imperative for National Reform. The report had an impact, wrote educators John D. Pulliam and James L. Van Patten, "similar to that of Sputnik in 1957." According to Lou Cannon, it "sparked a national drive for educational excellence" and led to a competitive ranking of states in various categories of educational achievement.[37]

During his eight years in office, Reagan was not able to cut overall government spending, which remained at roughly 22 percent of GDP. But the change in priorities was significant, with defense spending increasing to 6 percent of GDP, enabling the president to deal with the Soviets from a position of strength. Even so, Heritage analysts Robert Rector and Michael Sanera pointed out that the Reagan buildup, measured in constant dollars, was "about the size of Eisenhower's peacetime military increases."[38]

When Reagan was directly challenged in a cabinet meeting that he "couldn't spend all of this money on the military" and that it would look bad to boost spending on guns while cutting the butter, he leaned forward and raised his hand. "Look, I am the President of the United States, the commander in chief. My primary responsibility is the security of the United States. . . . If we don't have our security, we'll have no need for social programs. We're going to go ahead with these [military] programs."[39] There were no more objections by cabinet members about the largest peacetime military buildup in American history. As Reagan repeatedly said, given what he regarded as "a perilous situation vis-à-vis the Soviets," he would always choose building up America's defenses over balancing the budget.[40]

If one examines the economic report cards of postwar American presidents from Truman through Reagan, Reagan easily finishes first. Using the change each year in inflation, unemployment, interest rates, and growth in gross national product, Harvard economist Robert Barro ranked Reagan number one. Among other things, Reagan engineered the largest reduction in the misery index (the total of inflation and unemployment) in history: 50 percent. In fact, sums up economist Richard B. McKenzie, the 1980s were, up to then, "the most prosperous decade in American history" in peacetime.[41]

The Legal Legacy

The 368 federal judges that Reagan appointed—constituting about half of the judiciary, more than any other president—constitute an enormous legacy. He also elevated conservative William H. Rehnquist to chief justice of the Supreme Court and appointed three associate justices, including the first woman, Sandra Day O'Connor. Almost as important as the Rehnquist appointment was that of Antonin Scalia, a U.S. Court of Appeals judge and a former scholar at the American Enterprise Institute, as an associate justice. Scalia has been unwavering and eloquent in his opposition to affirmative action, abortion, and what he calls the "liberal jurisprudence" that undergirds judicial activism.[42] Other appointments, including Douglas Ginsburg, Alex Kozinski, Kenneth Starr, and Danny Boggs, helped turn the tide of activism in many federal circuits.

As Reagan stated, his goal was a federal judiciary "made up of judges who believe in law and order and a strict interpretation of the Constitution." And like FDR, wrote political scientist Sheldon Goldman, Reagan "saw the federal judiciary as crucial to achieving a major part of his presidential agenda." Those in charge of the selection process, first attorney general William French Smith and then his successor Edwin Meese III, emphasized that the administration aimed "to institutionalize the Reagan revolution so that it can't be set aside no matter what happens in future presidential elections."[43]

President Reagan was able to persuade the Senate to approve most of his judicial nominations from 1981 to 1986 because, ever the fusionist, he forged a broad coalition among traditional conservatives like Strom Thurmond, chairman of the Senate Judiciary Committee; New Right conservatives like John East of North Carolina and Jeremiah Denton of Alabama; and moderate law-and-order Republicans like Arlen Specter of Pennsylvania. That coalition's effectiveness was severely diluted when Democrats regained control of the Senate in the elections of 1986 and named Joseph Biden of Delaware chairman of the Judiciary Committee.

Reagan's most dramatic judicial defeat came in 1987 when he nominated federal judge Robert Bork to the Supreme Court. Bork's confirmation was challenged by a well-organized network of liberal organizations like the American Civil Liberties Union (ACLU), People for the American Way, and the AFL-CIO. One analyst put the cost of the anti-Bork media campaign at an unprecedented $15 million.

Although the American Bar Association rated Bork "well qualified," the ACLU bluntly called him "unfit." Senator Edward Kennedy, who led the Senate fight against the conservative jurist, charged apocalyptically that confirmation of Bork would lead to an America where

[W]omen would be forced into back-alley abortions, blacks would sit at segregated lunch counters, rogue police would break down citizens' doors in midnight raids, school children would not be taught about evolution, writers and authors could be censored at the whim of government, and the doors of the federal courts would be shut on the fingers of millions of citizens.[44]

The Supreme Court correspondent of the *Boston Globe,* the senator's hometown newspaper, wrote that Kennedy "shamelessly twisted Bork's world view."[45]

Bork's nomination dominated the national political agenda in the late summer and early fall of 1987. His five days of testimony before the Senate Judiciary Committee were nationally televised. Former president Gerald Ford personally introduced the nominee to the committee, causing former president Jimmy Carter to send a letter stating his opposition. One hundred and ten witnesses appeared for and against Bork during two weeks of hearings. After the Democrat-controlled Judiciary Committee refused to recommend Bork, the Senate then voted 58 to 42 against confirmation. Shortly thereafter, Reagan nominated and won confirmation of Anthony M. Kennedy, a low-key moderate conservative, to the Supreme Court.

Although Bork's rejection was a major setback for the Reagan administration, it could not negate Reagan's legal legacy of a generally conservative federal judiciary from top to bottom. "Reagan's success lies not simply in quantity but quality," stated conservative author Terry Eastland, who worked in the administration's Justice Department. Reagan's judges, according to Lou Cannon, "ranked above [those of] Carter, Ford, Nixon and Johnson."[46] The president's appointments helped revive a jurisprudence of original intent grounded in the philosophy of the Founders and the written Constitution they bequeathed to us.

The 1980s were generally bountiful years for American conservatives as all the elements of a successful political movement came together: a coherent, relevant philosophy, a national constituency, requisite financing, a solid organizational base, media skill, and a charismatic, principled leader. At the center of the conservative movement was that remarkable political fusionist, Ronald Reagan, who brought together traditional conservatives, libertarians, and neoconservatives, evangelical Protestants and ethnic Catholics, southerners, Midwesterners, and Westerners, rock-ribbed Republicans, yellow-dog

Democrats, and prickly Independents. He did so by appealing, as he put it in his final Oval Office talk, to their best hopes, not their worst fears. He did so by reiterating traditional American themes of duty, honor, and country. "In his evocation of our national memory and symbols of pride," said education secretary William J. Bennett, "in his summoning us to our national purpose and to national greatness, he performed the crucial task of political leadership."[47]

Reagan was faithful to conservative ideas at a time when Americans were ready to listen to them and act on them. He framed the debate, as analyst Peter J. Ferrara pointed out, forcing his adversaries to respond to his proposals on taxes and spending. He forced the debate "to take place on his terms and his choices," which were, wherever possible, to lower taxes, cut government programs, eliminate regulations, and reduce government handouts.[48]

CHAPTER 7

The Reagan Doctrine

S INCE THE MID-1940S, the United States and its allies had
striven to contain communism around the world with a
series of diplomatic, military, and economic initiatives that
had cost tens of thousands of lives and hundreds of billions of dollars. And yet
communism was not only alive and seemingly well in the Soviet Union,
Eastern and Central Europe, Mainland China, Cuba, and North Korea but
had spread to sub-Saharan Africa, Afghanistan, and Nicaragua. Containment
was not working or at least not fast enough for the new president.

As Reagan told Richard Allen in January 1977, the time had come to
defeat communism. He took his lead from fellow conservative Barry
Goldwater, who had asked in his 1962 book, "Why not victory?" In his first
news conference as president, Reagan bluntly denounced the Soviet leadership as still dedicated to "world revolution and a one-world Socialist-
Communist state." As Reagan put it in his 1990 autobiography, "I decided
we had to send as powerful a message as we could to the Russians that we
weren't going to stand by anymore while they armed and financed terrorists and subverted democratic governments."[1]

The establishment, led by such luminaries as Arthur Schlesinger Jr. and
John Kenneth Galbraith, were appalled at such dangerous saber rattling.
The Soviet Union was economically strong and militarily powerful—the
only responsible policy was detente. After visiting Moscow in 1982,
Schlesinger declared: "Those in the U.S. who think the Soviet Union is on
the verge of economic and social collapse, ready with one small push to go
over the brink, are . . . only kidding themselves." Two years later, following
a two months' stay in Moscow, Galbraith published a glowing appraisal of
Soviet economics, stating that "the Soviet economy has made great national
progress in recent years."[2]

In truth, Mikhail Gorbachev took command in 1985 of a disintegrating empire. Some seventy years after the Bolshevik Revolution, Soviet economic growth was stagnant, farms were unable to feed the people, most factories never met their quotas or inflated their figures, consumers lined up for blocks in Moscow and other cities for the bare necessities, and the war in Afghanistan dragged on with no end in sight to the fighting or the deaths of thousands of young Soviet soldiers.

Based on intelligence reports and his own instincts, Reagan concluded that communism was cracking and ready to crumble. The president, according to David Wigg, the CIA liaison to the White House, "particularly enjoyed information about the economic troubles [the Soviets] were experiencing." But his interests went far beyond the economic. "What are [the Soviets] saying about the Pope in Warsaw?" he asked his national security adviser William Clark. "What is Leonid Brezhnev thinking about in Europe? How are they dealing with losses in Afghanistan?"[3] In his first year as president, Reagan chaired fifty-seven meetings of the National Security Council (NSC), more than one a week. Rarely in peacetime, wrote Peter Schweizer, had presidents sustained "such a pace of involvement in national security affairs."[4]

The president first went public with his daring prognosis of the Soviet Union's systemic weakness at his alma mater, Eureka College, in May 1982, declaring that the Soviet empire was "faltering because rigid centralized control has destroyed incentives for innovation, efficiency and individual achievement." One month later, in a prophetic address to British members of Parliament at Westminster, Reagan said that the Soviet Union was gripped by a "great revolutionary crisis" and that a "global campaign for freedom" would ultimately prevail. In one of the most memorable utterances of his presidency, Reagan predicted that "the march of freedom and democracy . . . will leave Marxism-Leninism on the ash-heap of history as it has left other tyrannies which stifle the freedom and muzzle the self-expression of the people."[5]

It was bold rhetoric and, according to most liberals and some conservatives, wishful thinking. The New York Times scorned the Westminster speech as an appeal for "flower power" and said that "curiously missing from his plan was any formula for using Western economic strength to promote political accommodation."[6] But Reagan did have a plan, although not the conciliatory one the Times had in mind.

The president directed his top national security team—CIA director William Casey, Defense Secretary Caspar Weinberger, National Security

Adviser Richard Allen, and his successor, William P. Clark, and Lawrence Eagleburger from the State Department—to develop a plan to end the Cold War by winning it. "We adopted a comprehensive strategy," Weinberger recalled, "that included economic warfare to attack Soviet weaknesses." It was an offensive strategy intended to shift "the focus of the superpower struggle" to the Soviet bloc and the Soviet Union itself.[7] Nothing this bold had ever been contemplated let alone attempted by the United States in all the years of the Cold War.

In early 1981, according to Peter Schweizer, the Pentagon convened a group of specialists, under the direction of Fred Ikle, the undersecretary of defense for policy. They produced a still classified "defense guidance" for resource and force planning that included two new objectives: (1) "Reverse the geographic expansion of Soviet control and military presence throughout the world," and (2) "Encourage long-term political and military changes within the Soviet empire."[8]

National Security Adviser Bill Clark directed Richard Pipes, the distinguished Harvard historian and Sovietologist, to draft a strategic plan consistent with Reagan's long-held view of seeking to end the Cold War by undermining the Soviet system. Pipes, who served on Reagan's NSC staff for two years, responded with a remarkable forty-three-page paper which argued that détente had been a "mistake" because it assumed that dealing with the Soviet leadership would persuade them to change their policy. To the contrary, said Pipes, Soviet aggressiveness was "inherent" in the system and what was necessary was to "change" the system. Pipes listed three key objectives: "(1) the decentralization and demilitarization of the Soviet economy; (2) the weakening of power and privileged position of the ruling communist elite; and (3) gradual democratization of the USSR."[9]

With these two strategic studies as a foundation, the president's vision was specifically implemented through a series of top-secret national security decision directives (NSDDs). NSDD-32, approved in March 1982, declared that the United States would seek to "neutralize" Soviet control over Eastern Europe and authorized the use of covert action and other means to support anti-Soviet groups in the region. In November 1982, NSDD-66, drafted by NSC aide Roger Robinson, stated that it would be U.S. policy to disrupt the Soviet economy by attacking a "strategic triad" of critical resources—financial credits, high technology, and natural gas—deemed essential to Soviet economic survival. NSDD-66 was tantamount, Robinson later said, "to a secret declaration of economic war on the Soviet Union."[10]

The third directive was NSDD-75, written by Pipes. Issued in January 1983, it called for the United States no longer to coexist with the Soviet system but rather to seek to change it fundamentally, something that George Kennan, the author of containment, did not think was possible. NSDD-75 "was a clear break from the past," said Pipes. "At its root was the belief that we had in our power to alter the Soviet system through the use of external pressure." The directive's language was unequivocal—America intended to roll back Soviet influence at every opportunity.[11]

Taking its lead from these three NSDDs, the Reagan administration pursued a multifaceted foreign policy offensive that included covert and other support to the Solidarity movement in Poland, a psychological operation to engender indecision and fear among Soviet leaders along with an increase in pro-freedom public diplomacy, a global campaign to reduce Soviet access to Western high technology, and a drive to hurt the Soviet economy by driving down the price of oil and limiting natural gas exports to the West.

Naming the Doctrine

The Reagan Doctrine was the name given to Reagan's already functioning but top-secret foreign policy by neoconservative columnist Charles Krauthammer. In an April 1985 article, he wrote:

> The Reagan Doctrine proclaims overt and unashamed support for anticommunist revolution. . . . It is intended to establish a new, firmer—a doctrinal—foundation for such support by declaring equally worthy all armed resistance to communism whether foreign or indigenously imposed.[12]

Krauthammer had no way of knowing that Pipes, Robinson, and other security aides had already said much the same in NSDD-32, NSDD-66, and NSDD-75. In keeping with their boss's injunction not to worry who gets the credit so long as things get done, Reagan aides allowed Krauthammer to remain the man who "invented" the Reagan Doctrine.[13] But none of the more than two hundred NSDDs that the president signed referred to a "Reagan Doctrine." In truth, Reagan's strategy was far more complex than Krauthammer's conception, which was essentially a policy of proxy warfare in four countries—Afghanistan, Nicaragua, Angola, and Cambodia.

But the importance of the Reagan administration's decision to assist pro-freedom, anticommunist forces in these countries should not be underestimated. To his credit, President Carter had begun helping the anti-Soviet *mujahideen* in Afghanistan during his final months in office. But American aid to what Reagan called "freedom fighters" increased significantly during his administration. A key decision was the White House approval of Stinger ground-to-air missiles, which the *mujahideen* desperately needed and promptly used to shoot down the Soviet Hind helicopters that had kept them on the defensive. "Do whatever you have to do to help the *mujahideen*," Reagan told his national security advisers, "not only to survive but to *win*."[14]

Across the Atlantic Ocean, the Marxist Sandinistas were not only establishing a Leninist state in Nicaragua but were supporting communist guerrillas in El Salvador and elsewhere. Concerned about the spread of communism throughout the region, the Reagan administration directed the CIA to form an anti-Sandinista movement and then asked Congress to approve funds for the contras, as they were called, when ten thousand peasants joined them.

The president cared deeply about the future of Central America. When House Speaker Tip O'Neill kept insisting that he and others in Congress would block the administration's program, Reagan privately exploded: "The Sandinistas have openly proclaimed Communism in their country and their support of Marxist revolution throughout Central America . . . they're killing and torturing people! Now what the hell does Congress expect me to do about that?"[15]

Reagan, however, never contemplated sending U.S. troops to Nicaragua. He believed that with sufficient military support and firm diplomatic negotiation, Nicaraguans could rid themselves of the Marxist regime. He was proved correct by the democratic elections in February 1990 when anti-Sandinista Violeta Chamorro decisively defeated Sandinista commandante Daniel Ortega for president.

In another part of the world, when Soviet-backed forces formed a government in Angola in sub-Saharan Africa, the United States promptly allied itself with the anticommunist Union for the Total National Independence of Angola (UNITA), led by Jonas Savimbi. The Reagan administration began helping UNITA in 1985 when congressional proscriptions on assistance were lifted.

And in Asia, after Pol Pot of the murderous Khmer Rouge had wiped out as much as one-fourth of the Cambodian population in the mid-1970s, he was overthrown by a puppet regime installed by the communist government of Vietnam. A guerrilla movement then emerged in Cambodia, including elements of the old Sihanouk monarchy, some democrats, and the Khmer Rouge itself. In this constantly shifting situation, the Reagan administration supported the insurgents, while trying to minimize help to the Khmer Rouge.

As applied in these four countries, the Reagan Doctrine was the most cost-effective of all the cold war doctrines, costing the United States only an estimated half-billion dollars a year and yet forcing the cash-strapped Soviets to spend some $8 billion annually to deflect the impact. The doctrine was also one of the most politically successful in Cold War history. It resulted in a Soviet pullout from Afghanistan, the election of a democratic government in Nicaragua, and the removal of forty thousand Cuban troops from Angola and the holding of UN-monitored elections there. Only in Cambodia was the result less than satisfactory: former Khmer Rouge officials continued to dominate the government, although in 1997 Pol Pot was captured and scheduled to be tried for crimes against the Cambodian people before his death in 1998.

For President Reagan, 1983 was a pivotal year. In March, before a group of evangelical ministers, the president stated that the West should recognize that the Soviets "are the focus of evil in this modern world" and the masters of "an evil empire." Many consider Reagan's "evil empire" speech the most important of his presidency, a compelling example of what former Czech president Vaclav Havel calls "the power of words to change history." When Reagan visited Poland and East Germany in September 1990 after the collapse of communism in Eastern Europe, former dissidents told him that when he called the Soviet Union an "evil empire," it gave them enormous hope. Finally, they said to each other, America had a leader who "understood the nature of communism."[16]

The reaction of American liberals was not so favorable, with the historian Henry Steele Commager asserting, "It was the worst presidential speech in American history, and I've read them all." George Ball, a high-ranking State Department official in both the Kennedy and Johnson administrations, later published an open letter to Reagan in which he excoriated the president's "obsessive detestation of what you call the 'evil empire.'" From the

Right, William F. Buckley Jr. made an intriguing comparison between Reagan's speech and Lincoln's second inaugural with its references to America's own "legacy of evil"—slavery. Each president, said Buckley, when confronted with unquestionable iniquity, judged it necessary to acknowledge and condemn the evil, even if in so doing they disturbed and even angered others. In effect, suggests political scientist Paul Kengor, Reagan was laying the philosophical groundwork for a "just war"—cold though it may have been—with the Soviets.[17]

The president acted decisively whenever the Soviets tried to extend their empire. In October 1983, Reagan dispatched two thousand American troops, along with military units from six Caribbean states, to the island of Grenada to oust a Marxist regime that had recently seized power. It was the first time in nearly forty years of the Cold War that America had acted to restore democracy to a communist country. The once-sacrosanct Brezhnev Doctrine—once a communist state, always a communist state—was successfully challenged.

The *New York Times* complained editorially that the Grenada invasion was "a reverberating demonstration to the world that America has no more respect for laws and borders, for the codes of civilization, than the Soviet Union." But a bipartisan congressional delegation visited Grenada shortly thereafter, and nearly every member, including critical Democrats, reported that after talking to Grenadians and inspecting the warehouses filled with Cuban weapons, they "agreed with the president" on his action.[18] Subsequently, American troops uncovered a hoard of documents detailing the Marxist regime's secret arms pacts with other communist countries—three with the Soviet Union, one each with Cuba and North Korea—and "its plans to make the island a military base for Soviet bloc activities" throughout the Caribbean.[19]

That fall, despite carefully coordinated protests in the streets of London, Rome, Paris, and other European cities, the Reagan administration proceeded with the deployment of Pershing II and cruise missiles in Western Europe. They were deployed because the Soviets had installed several hundred SS-20s (intermediate-range nuclear missiles) aimed at key points in West Germany and other NATO countries.

Reagan had given Moscow a "zero option"—either to dismantle all the SS-20s or accept the deployment of American missiles directed at major Soviet targets. The Soviets had refused to dismantle, gambling they could apply enough pressure through diplomatic maneuvers and the nuclear freeze movement in Western Europe and the United States to force Reagan to cancel deployment. They had yet to take the full measure of the American president.

The stakes were high in Europe. Six Western European countries had scheduled elections for 1983—Great Britain, the Federal Republic of Germany, Italy, Belgium, Norway, and the Netherlands—and in each of these countries, as political scientists Andrew E. Busch and Elizabeth Spalding have written, "the leading liberal-left party had been captured by the peace movement and was opposing INF deployment."[20] Had voters turned against deployment, the NATO alliance would have been seriously weakened, but backed by Western leadership, every one of the European parties that stood for military preparedness won that year. As British prime minister Margaret Thatcher noted, Reagan "strengthened not only America's defenses, but also the will of America's allies."[21]

Reagan predicted that eventually the Soviets would come to the bargaining table. And so they did four years later when the Intermediate-Range Nuclear Forces (INF) Treaty of 1987 was signed by President Reagan and Premier Mikhail Gorbachev. Never before in the Cold War had an entire category of nuclear weapons been eliminated. Gorbachev's signature confirmed Reagan's shrewd judgment of him, which had been questioned by some hardline anticommunists. Reagan insisted that Gorbachev was "different" from previous Soviet leaders and "a remarkable force for change." His insightful evaluation was supported by Margaret Thatcher, who pronounced after her first meeting with Gorbachev, "We can do business together."[22] Some American conservatives—including William F. Buckley Jr. and the editors of *Human Events*—did not like the sound of that, but the White House responded that the president's reference to a "new" Soviet leadership would be proved or disproved quickly. Would Soviet weapons "continue to pour into Nicaragua?" Would troops be "pulled out of Afghanistan?"[23]

Scarcely a year later, the Soviets had pulled their forces out of Afghanistan, and sharply reduced their support of their Marxist protégés in Nicaragua.

In his four summit meetings with Gorbachev, Reagan encouraged an open dialogue but never conceded an important point. At their first meeting in Geneva, for example, the two leaders with only their interpreters present sat before a fire exchanging pleasantries and talking about children. At last, Reagan looked Gorbachev directly into his eyes and in what he later called a "plaintive, wistful tone" said, "I do hope for the sake of our children that we can find some way to avert this terrible, escalating arms race." Reagan paused, and Gorbachev smiled slyly, unable to mask a look of triumph, but before he could respond, Reagan continued, "Because if we can't, America will not lose it, I assure you."[24]

The Most Important Initiative

And then there was the Strategic Defense Initiative (SDI). Reagan had long favored an alternative to the policy of mutual assured destruction (MAD), under which the United States and the Soviet Union each retained the nuclear capability to retaliate and destroy the other in the event of a nuclear attack. MAD was based on the assumption, as Caspar Weinberger put it, that in the area of nuclear strategy, the Soviet Union would act as the United States would act: "they would take no risks we would not." Proponents explained that mutual vulnerability was a vital precondition to MAD. That is, both sides would be safe because both were vulnerable. Weinberger was less diplomatic; he called MAD a "mutual suicide pact."[25]

Reagan apparently first encountered the idea of missile defense in 1967 when he visited Edward Teller, the father of the hydrogen bomb, in the Lawrence Livermore National Laboratory in California. Teller briefed the new governor about the work being done to stop a missile attack on the United States. "It was a rather long presentation," Teller later recalled, "and I remember clearly that [Reagan] listened quite attentively." Some day, said Teller, space-based lasers might be used to destroy nuclear missiles fired at the United States. Reagan responded that history showed that "all offensive weapons eventually met their match through defense countermeasures."[26]

In 1976, when he was challenging Gerald Ford for the Republican presidential nomination, Reagan often expressed his doubts about the MAD doctrine. Daniel O. Graham, the former director of the Defense Intelligence Agency and then a national security adviser to the conservative candidate, recalled that Reagan put it this way: "Our nuclear policy is like a Mexican stand-off—two men with pistols pointed at each other's head. If the man's finger flinches, you each blow the other's brains out. Can't you military people come up with something better than *that*?"[27]

Still looking for an answer, Reagan in July 1979 toured the headquarters of the North American Aerospace Defense Command (NORAD) in

Colorado. He asked air force general James Hill what could be done if the Soviets fired a missile at an American city. Nothing, Hill admitted. All NORAD could do was track the incoming missile and then give city officials ten to fifteen minutes' warning before it hit. The soon-to-be presidential candidate found it hard to accept that after three decades of the Cold War, the United States still had no defense whatever against Soviet missiles. Reagan kept pushing for an alternative to MAD. It turned out to be the SDI, about which the normally modest president said flatly, "SDI was my idea."[28]

There was opposition to SDI throughout the Reagan administration. Once, with Reagan present, Secretary of State George Shultz called the president's science adviser, George Keyworth, "a lunatic" for his advocacy of SDI, arguing that it would "destroy" NATO. But Reagan did not budge from his commitment, causing an admiring Keyworth to remark that Reagan "has this marvelous ability to work the whole thing while everybody else is working the parts."[29]

On March 23, 1983, President Reagan announced in a nationally televised address (drafted by National Security Adviser Robert McFarlane) that development and deployment of a comprehensive antiballistic missile system would be his top defense priority—his "ultimate goal." "I call upon the scientific community in our country," he said, "those who gave us nuclear weapons, to turn their great talents now to the cause of mankind and world peace, to give us the means of rendering these nuclear weapons impotent and obsolete." SDI was immediately ridiculed as "Star Wars" by liberal detractors, led by Senator Edward Kennedy. The *New York Times* called the initiative "a pipe dream, a projection of fantasy into policy."[30]

The Soviets, led by General Secretary Yuri Andropov, protested that SDI was a "strike weapon" and a preparation for the launching of a U.S. nuclear attack inasmuch as it would nullify any Soviet response. They warned that SDI would force an expensive arms race in space, at the end of which the strategic balance would remain the same despite the enormous expenditures.[31] Moscow's intense opposition to SDI showed that Soviet scientists regarded the initiative not as pipe dream but a technological feat they could not match. General Vladimir Slipchenko, a leading military scientist who served on the Soviet General Staff, recalled that SDI put the military "in a state of fear and shock." A decade later, General Makhmut Gareev, who headed the department of strategic analysis in the Soviet Ministry of

Defense, revealed what he had told the Soviet general staff and the Politburo in 1983: "Not only could we not defeat SDI, SDI defeated all our possible countermeasures."[32]

More than any other strategic action he took, Reagan's unwavering commitment to SDI convinced the Kremlin it could not win, or afford, a continuing arms race and led Gorbachev to sue for peace and end the cold war peacefully. As Alexander Solzhenitsyn said, Gorbachev "had no choice but to disarm."[33]

Another application of Reagan's offensive strategy was the barrage of measures aimed at the Soviet-backed regime of General Wojciech Jaruzelski in Poland. The administration worked closely with the AFL-CIO, headed by veteran anticommunist Lane Kirkland, and the Vatican to provide the political movement Solidarity with money, literature, and electronic and communications equipment. When Reagan and Pope John Paul II met in Rome in early 1982, they formed what an observer called a "holy alliance" against communism in Eastern and Central Europe. "Hope remains in Poland," Reagan said to the Pontiff. "We, working together, can keep it alive." The Pope nodded in agreement. Solidarity leader Lech Walesa said later that the movement would not have survived without American help, overt and covert. Asked, for example, how important Radio Free Europe and other Western media had been, he replied, "Would there be the earth without the sun?"[34]

Essential to the success of the Reagan Doctrine in Poland was the quasi-public National Endowment for Democracy (NED). Evolving from an idea first proposed by academic Constantine Menges—who later served on Reagan's National Security Council staff—NED had a mandate to support democratic movements around the world. But Poland was accorded the highest priority. The endowment funded an East European Democracy Project, which published books and materials that were then smuggled into Poland, reducing communist control over information. United States funds were also used to purchase paper, equipment, spare parts, and printing supplies for underground publications inside Poland. Sometimes getting material behind the Iron Curtain required creative thinking. Once some ten thousand balloons carrying containers of anti-Soviet, pro-Solidarity propaganda leaflets were released from an island in Denmark to ride the wind into Poland.[35]

Meanwhile Libya, under military dictator Muammar Qaddafi, had built up an arsenal of Soviet-made weapons and openly taunted the United States. Following a Libyan-inspired terrorist attack on a Berlin nightclub, in which several Americans were killed, Reagan acted decisively: He ordered American planes in April 1986 to bomb Libya, calling Qaddafi the "mad dog of the Middle East." The American public overwhelmingly endorsed Reagan's action, which had the desired effect. The Libyan leader immediately muted his criticism of the United States and backed away from further terrorist actions.[36] Foreign policy experts have credited Reagan with laying the groundwork for Qaddafi's unexpected announcement in 2003 that he would eliminate all of his country's weapons of mass destruction (WMD) and his invitation to U.N. inspectors to supervise and corroborate his actions.

On the Offensive

Throughout the 1970s, America had retreated almost everywhere in the world—in Vietnam, Laos, Cambodia, Angola, Ethiopia, Nicaragua, and before the OPEC oil cartel. It turned over the Panama Canal, accepted Soviet violations of treaties like SALT I, encouraged the Soviets to invade Afghanistan by its indecisiveness and timidity, and allowed the overthrow of the Shah of Iran, a good friend, and vital ally.

But in the 1980s, America once again became the leader of the free world. It did so because Reagan rebuilt America's military arsenal, worked closely with Western allies on consequential security issues like the deployment of Euromissiles, and successfully challenged the Brezhnev Doctrine in Grenada, Angola, Afghanistan, and Nicaragua. America demonstrated it would fulfill its commitments to allies in Western Europe, Japan, Israel, and Southeast Asia.

Reagan took his freedom offensive into the heart of the disintegrating Soviet empire. Standing before Berlin's Brandenburg Gate in June 1987, Reagan directly challenged the Kremlin, proclaiming, "Mr. Gorbachev, tear down this wall!" His blunt words were a telling contrast to John F. Kennedy's emotional but essentially reactive declaration a quarter of a century earlier, "Ich bin ein Berliner," which thrilled the people of West Berlin but was ignored by Soviet leaders.[37] White House aide Peter Robinson, who drafted the Berlin Wall speech, has recounted how the State Department and the National Security Council fought for three weeks to delete what they considered to be crude and overly provocative language. When President Reagan was asked what he wanted to say to the people "on the other side of the Berlin Wall," he replied, "That Wall has to come down. That's what I'd like to say."[38] And so he did.

Reagan's challenge at the Brandenburg Gate was part of his strategy to force the Soviet Union to make fundamental challenges or become obsolete. "Gorbachev saw the handwriting on the Wall," Reagan wrote in his memoir, "and opted for change"—change that, although the Soviet leader did not realize it, would bring about an end to Soviet communism.[39]

By introducing such populist concepts as *glasnost* and *perestroika,* Gorbachev made consideration of the people potentially as important as the traditional components of the Soviet state: the Communist Party, the KGB, the Soviet army, and the *nomenklatura.* For his reforms to work, Gorbachev had to replace old ways with new ways of thinking, and that required diversity, debate, and freedom, long absent from the Soviet Union. He gambled that he could control the virus of freedom he had let loose with *glasnost;* improve the economy and satisfy the consumer desires of the people through *perestroika;* reassure the military and the KGB he was not jeopardizing their role; persuade the *nomenklatura* to relax its grip on the machinery of the state; secure his own position as general secretary of the Communist Party; and keep the Soviet Union socialist.

Gorbachev was probably not familiar with Alexis de Tocqueville, who wrote, "Experience teaches us that the most critical moment for bad governments is the one which witnesses the first steps toward reform."[40] The Soviet Union in the mid-1980s was a very bad government attempting very radical reform. Gorbachev was trying to square a circle—democratize a totalitarian state—and manipulate an elemental human force, freedom, that has proved to be the downfall of every dictator sooner or later.

Resolved to bring about that downfall sooner, Reagan traveled to Moscow in the spring of 1988 for what biographer Lou Cannon described as his premier presidential performance as freedom's advocate. Beneath a gigantic white bust of Lenin at Moscow State University, the president delivered a stirring speech on the blessings of democracy, individual freedom, and free enterprise. He explained that "freedom is the right to question and change the established way of doing things." He lauded the "continuing revolution of the marketplace" and the right "to follow your dream or stick to your conscience, even if you're the only one in a sea of doubters." He declared that America had always sought to make friends of old antagonists and suggested it was time for Americans and Russians to become friends:

In this Moscow spring, this May 1988, we may be allowed [this] hope: that freedom, like the fresh green sapling planted over

Tolstoy's grave, will blossom forth at last in the rich fertile soil of your people and culture. We may be allowed to hope that the marvelous sound of a new openness will keep rising, ringing through, to leading to a new world of reconciliation, friendship and peace.[41]

The key word that day and throughout his visit was *freedom*. Whether talking to about one hundred dissidents at the U.S. Embassy or in a broadcast to the Soviet people, Reagan's agenda was one of freedom of religion, freedom of speech, freedom to travel. Near the conclusion of his university talk, Reagan quoted the poet Alexander Pushkin, beloved above all others by Russians: "It's time, my friend, it's time."[42]

Democracy triumphed in the Cold War, Reagan wrote in his autobiography, because it was a battle of ideas—"between one system that gave preeminence to the state and another that gave preeminence to the individual and freedom."[43] The Cold War was indeed a triumph for the idea of freedom, and not, as some American academics and journalists would have it, for *realpolitik*.

The Scandal

Iran-contra had its origins in two quite different but essential impulses of Reagan. The first was humanitarian: to free the handful of American hostages held by terrorists in Lebanon. The second was ideological: to support the anticommunist resistance in Nicaragua, where a Marxist regime threatened stability in all of Central America and even beyond.

But exchanging arms for hostages contradicted the administration's stated policy of not acquiescing to the demands of terrorists or dealing with a state like Iran, which had been publicly identified as a key supporter of the terrorist group Hezbollah. Both Secretary of State Shultz and Defense Secretary Weinberger were adamantly opposed to any dealings with terrorists, but NSC staffers believed that moderate elements in Iran could help facilitate the release of the Americans being held in Lebanon. "Reagan was determined to get the hostages out," wrote Lou Cannon, "by whatever means possible." Indeed, the president became "so stubbornly committed to the trade of arms for hostages" that he could not be dissuaded from it even when new American hostages were taken."[44]

As Reagan put it in his memoir:

What American trapped in such circumstances wouldn't have wanted me to do everything I possibly could to set them free. . . . It was the president's *duty* to get them home.[45]

And so the president decided at the end of 1985 to proceed with the Iranian initiative. His decision sharply divided his top advisers, with Ed Meese, CIA director William Casey, and National Security Adviser John Poindexter in favor, and Shultz and Weinberger vehemently against it. One year later, the Reagan administration was struggling to contain a serious political crisis that critics regarded as equal to Nixon's Watergate. In March 1987, a very reluctant Reagan conceded in a nationally televised address, "A few months ago, I told the American people I did not trade arms for hostages. My heart and my best intentions still tell me that's true, but the facts and the evidence tell me it is not. . . . I let my personal concern for the hostages spill over into the geopolitical strategy of reaching out to Iran."[46]

Conservatives were stunned by the admission. Commented one Reagan appointee, "It's like suddenly learning that John Wayne had secretly been selling liquor and firearms to the Indians." Casting about for comparisons, the president wrote to his old friend Laurence Beilenson that the arms involved were $12 million worth of spare parts and antitank missiles while countries in Western Europe had sold almost $3 billion worth of weapons to Iran.[47] But even the ever faithful Meese admits that when it became clear that the initiative to build ties with Iranian "moderates" was not succeeding, "it should have been dropped and Congress should have been notified of what had happened." Meese, attorney general during Iran-contra, did not try to defend "the protracted failure to disclose" the administration's actions to Congress—as required by law—but argued that the sale of arms was "a policy error, not a crime."[48]

The American public was unequivocal in its rejection of any arms-for-hostages deal (the year-long occupation of the U.S. Embassy in Tehran was still fresh in most people's minds). A December 1986 *New York Times*/CBS News poll recorded a drop in Reagan's approval rating of twenty-one points, from 67 percent to 46 percent, the sharpest one-month drop in presidential surveys since such polling began in 1936.

The contra half of the scandal began in March 1982 when Congress discovered that the CIA was involved in training anticommunist rebels in Nicaragua. Led by Democratic House Speaker Tip O'Neill, Congress passed, in the fall of 1982, the first Boland amendment, which prohibited funds "for the purpose of overthrowing the government of Nicaragua." The Reagan administration argued that the goal of contra funding was not to overthrow the Sandinista government but to persuade it to hold democratic elections (which it finally, though reluctantly, did in 1990).[49]

Nicaragua was not a peripheral issue for either the administration or its critics. For Reagan, Nicaragua was another Cuba; for the Democratic leadership in Congress, it was another Vietnam. Believing that the vital interests of the nation were at stake, each side dug in hard and prepared for political war.

American funding of the contras continued until December 1984, when Congress strengthened the Boland Amendment by denying any U.S. support either "directly or indirectly" to the contras. Because the president wanted to keep helping what he called the "freedom fighters," administration lawyers decided that although Boland prohibited American agencies "engaged in intelligence activities" from operating in Nicaragua, the NSC was not an intelligence agency. So the pro-contra effort was shifted from the CIA to the NSC under the direction of National Security Adviser John Poindexter and NSC staffer Oliver North.[50]

Apparently with CIA director William Casey's approval, North illegally diverted profits from the Iranian arms sales to the contras. Meese called the fund diversion "a tremendous error that should never have been allowed to happen. That it did happen was a failure of the administration—for which it paid dearly."[51]

Ultimately, North, Poindexter, former national security adviser Robert McFarlane (who had succeeded William Clark), and General Richard Secord (who had bought weapons to trade for American hostages) were indicted and convicted on charges stemming from the Iran-contra affair. Many of the convictions were later overturned because independent counsel Lawrence Walsh had relied on information obtained by congressional investigators operating under grants of immunity to obtain his convictions.

But Iran-contra was not Watergate redux. Reagan did not try to cover up the affair but directed his attorney general to conduct an immediate and thorough inquiry. He invited former senators John Tower, a Republican, and Edmund Muskie, a Democrat, and Nixon's national security adviser, Brent Scowcroft, to undertake an independent investigation. And he asked for the appointment of an independent prosecutor to determine if any laws had been broken.

Unlike Nixon, Reagan did not approve wiretaps, did not direct the IRS to examine people's tax returns, did not suggest that offices be broken into, did not compile an enemies' list, and did not attempt to manipulate the FBI and the CIA in their investigations. However mistaken, Iran-contra was concerned with public policy; Watergate was always about electoral politics. Reagan approved the arms-for-hostages deal to save American lives; Nixon tried to contain the Watergate scandal to save himself.

Every official inquiry agreed that President Reagan had not personally authorized the diversion of money to the contras. The Tower Commission report found that the president had not even known of the diversion. Reagan wrote an old friend that "the money transfer" was "a complete surprise" to him. But the Tower Commission was highly critical of McFarlane and Poindexter, stating that the "National Security Adviser failed in his responsibility to see that an orderly process was observed."[52]

In November 1987, a select committee of the House and Senate released a seven-hundred-page report. Like the Tower Commission, the Democratic majority concluded that the president had been unaware of the funds diversion. It accepted Poindexter's testimony that "he shielded the president from knowledge of the diversion." The Republican minority emphasized that the mistakes of the Iran-contra affair were just that: "mistakes in judgment and nothing more. There was no constitutional crisis, no systematic disrespect for the 'internal rule of law,' no grand conspiracy."[53] Iran-contra soon faded from the public's consciousness as most Americans decided that it was an exception rather the rule of the Reagan Doctrine. The people gave Reagan "the benefit of the doubt," said longtime political adviser Stuart Spencer. "He made a goddamn mistake, now let's go on."[54]

The Age of Reagan

"No president save FDR," wrote Lou Cannon, "defined a decade as strikingly as Ronald Reagan defined the 1980s."[55] In fact, Reagan left an indelible mark on American politics, starting in the 1960s when he was governor of California, blossoming through the eight years of his presidency, and continuing to this day. Indeed, even as the first half of the twentieth century is usually called the Age of Roosevelt by American historians, I believe that the last half of the century will be called the Age of Reagan.

Ronald Reagan deliberately patterned his presidency after that of his favorite president, Franklin Delano Roosevelt. Just as FDR led America out of a great economic depression through his dynamic leadership and inspiring language, Reagan lifted a traumatized country out of a great psychological depression, induced by the assassinations of John F. Kennedy, Martin Luther King Jr., and Robert F. Kennedy, and sustained by the Vietnam War, Watergate, and the Carter malaise. And even as Roosevelt led America and the world to victory in World War II, Reagan led the nation and the free world to victory in another global conflict, the Cold War.

He used the same political instruments as Roosevelt—the major address to Congress and the fireside chat with the people—and the same optimistic, uplifting rhetoric. A favorite device of Reagan's was the five-minute Saturday radio broadcast; between April 1982 and January 1989, he delivered 331 radio talks on the issues of the day. But there was a major philosophical difference between the two presidents: Roosevelt turned first to government to solve problems, while Reagan turned first to the people. Reagan persuaded Americans to believe in themselves and the future again. He led them to accept that they did not need the federal government to solve all of their economic and social problems. He called the people "keepers of a miracle"—the American experiment in freedom.[56]

He was right about the resilience of Americans. It therefore came as no great surprise to anyone, including the Democrats, that Reagan was reelected in 1984 by an electoral landslide even greater than that of Lyndon Johnson twenty years earlier. Reagan received almost 59 percent of the popular vote and 525 electoral votes, carrying forty-nine states. With his overwhelming victory, summed up *Congressional Quarterly*, Reagan "ripped apart what was left of the once-dominant Democratic coalition," demonstrating that the GOP, at least at the presidential level, was the "real" umbrella party.[57] The only electoral cloud for the Republicans was their disappointing showing in Congress, where they gained only fourteen seats in the House and lost two seats in the Senate, reducing their majority there to 53-47.

The 1984 election was never in question, although a few doubts were raised following the president's poor performance in the first televised debate with Democratic candidate Walter Mondale. Reagan had repeated himself, sometimes sounded uncertain, and even looked old at times. No one had to tell Reagan what had happened: the old pro knew that he had flopped.

There were some excuses about the president's being "overbriefed," but a more pertinent reason was that Reagan had not debated anyone for years, and his skill at political thrust and parry had grown rusty. The campaign staff had not helped by shielding Reagan from the press and the public, and it was now decided to let Reagan be Reagan. A tough anti-Mondale speech was delivered with relish by the president. He revealed that he had become angry when Mondale kept distorting his record during their first debate and had thought of saying to his opponent, "You are taxing my patience." But then, said Reagan, "I caught myself. Why should I give him another idea? That's the only tax he hasn't thought of." The crowds loved it and chanted, "Four more years! Four more years!"[58]

When campaign consultant Roger Ailes (the future head of Fox News) warned the president that the age issue would probably be raised in the second debate, Reagan thought for a moment, smiled, and said, "I can handle that."[59] Thirty minutes into the debate, the *Baltimore Sun*'s Henry Trewhitt, a member of the journalists' panel, pointed out that Reagan was the oldest president in U.S. history and noted that some members of the president's staff had said he was tired after the first debate. "I recall," said Trewhitt, "that President Kennedy had to go for days on end with very little sleep during the Cuban missile crisis. Is there any doubt in your mind that you would be able to function in such circumstances?"

"Not at all, Mr. Trewhitt," replied Reagan calmly. "And I want you to know that also I will not make age an issue of this campaign." Absolutely deadpan, he added, "I am not going to exploit, for political purposes, my opponent's youth and inexperience."[60] Everyone, including Mondale, laughed, and for all practical purposes the 1984 presidential election was over. But the cognitive dissonance of the liberal establishment persisted. A few days before Reagan's triumphant reelection, the *New York Times*'s James Reston wrote that never before had so many journalists, editors, producers, and broadcasters done so much to defeat a candidate as they had to defeat Reagan, but "alas" they had failed.[61]

Reagan's dominance of American politics was confirmed four years later when George H. W. Bush was easily elected president in large part because he gave the electorate one more opportunity to vote for Ronald Reagan. American presidents are not always so successful in transferring their popularity as Eisenhower learned in 1960 and Bill Clinton in 2000. Although it was not a Reaganesque landslide, Bush received 53.4 percent of the popular vote and carried forty states, giving him a decisive 426 to 112 triumph over Michael Dukakis in the Electoral College. Bush swept the South, the Rocky Mountains, much of the farm belt, and every large state except New York.

Reagan left office with a final public approval rating of 63 percent, the highest of any president up to that point—surpassed later only by Bill Clinton, who received a final Gallup rating of 68 percent. The *New York Times*/CBS News poll gave Reagan an approval rating of 68 percent in January 1989— 71 percent supported his handling of foreign relations. In June 2004, when Gallup asked recipients whether presidents Nixon, Carter, Reagan, George H. W. Bush, Clinton, and George W. Bush should be described as outstanding or above average, Reagan led with a combined rating of 58 percent—Clinton was second with 38 percent. That was up four points from an August 1999 Gallup survey in which 54 percent responded that Reagan would be remembered as an "outstanding" or "above average" president.

Reagan averaged a 53 percent job approval rating during his presidency, which was higher than the averages of his three immediate predecessors— Jimmy Carter, Gerald Ford, and Richard Nixon—but lower than that of three earlier presidents—Lyndon Johnson, John F. Kennedy, and Dwight D. Eisenhower.[62] His average was dragged down by the concerns about the economy in 1981 and 1982 and Iran-contra in 1987. Two final Gallup statistics: when the public was asked in November 2003, in an open-ended format, who was the greatest U.S. president, Reagan placed third, behind John Kennedy and Abraham Lincoln. And from 1974 to 2003, Reagan appeared in the top ten most admired men every year. His thirty-one appearances were second only to Billy Graham.[63]

But when leading academics were asked to describe Reagan's legacy, they were often condescending and dismissive. In the spring of 1988, while Reagan was still in the White House and implementing his "freedom" campaign in the Soviet Union, Arthur Schlesinger Jr., the dean of American historians wrote:

> A few years from now, I believe, Reaganism will seem a weird and improbable memory, a strange interlude of national hallucination, rather as the McCarthyism of the early 1950s and the youth rebellion of the late 1960s appear to us today.[64]

It would be difficult to find a more errant analysis of the Reagan years— Weird memory? National hallucination? McCarthyism?—unless you read the academic literature about Ronald Reagan. Many professors are unable to get past the Hollywood years and the cowboy image to consider objectively what the man accomplished and why.

Representative of collegiate textbooks is *Reaganism and the Death of Representative Democracy* by Walter Williams, a professor of government at the University of Washington, who says flatly that "President Reagan's policies did more harm than good and were particularly damaging in materially increasing the maldistribution of income and wealth." He charges that "Reaganomics" did not stimulate the nineties' "boom" and would have in fact deterred the strong economic growth if George H. W. Bush and Bill Clinton "had not enacted major tax increases."[65]

In *The Reagan Presidency: Pragmatic Conservatism and Its Legacies,* political scientist Samuel Wells says that Reagan won Gorbachev's "agreement" not through a decisive military buildup and a steadfast commitment to the SDI but through what he calls "concessions." The book ends with a sour summing up by the respected historian James Patterson, who writes that Reagan did not succeed in resisting the tide of Big Government. Nor did he "shove politics and political thinking toward the Right" as Franklin D. Roosevelt moved the nation toward the Left in the 1930s. To speak of a "Reagan Revolution" is excessive, Patterson insists: such "grand phrases" should be reserved for presidents like FDR and Harry Truman.[66]

As Emory University professor Harvey Klehr puts it, a "significant cadre of historians cannot abide the idea that the United States won the Cold War." Bruce Cummings of the University of Chicago, for example, doesn't think it was much of a battle: the United States did not defeat "a worthy adversary" but rather "a defensive and brittle movement."[67] Writing in the *Washington Post* less than one month after Reagan's death, George Washington University's James Hershberg posited that Mikhail Gorbachev was the "one who mattered most" in bringing down the Soviet Union. Hershberg disposes of Reagan's various initiatives—arming the *mujahideen* in Afghanistan, backing the contras in Nicaragua, building up the American military—as either begun by others or peripheral influences on the outcome of the conflict. Aside from Gorbachev, Hershberg accords "much credit" for winning the Cold War to the Beatles and such giants of Western counterculture as Frank Zappa, Pink Floyd, Lou Reed, and James Dean.[68] Such revisionism while amusing is unlikely to have any lasting effect on serious historians of the future.

The academic evaluations of Reagan are not always all bad. Presidential scholar Fred Greenstein finds the Reagan presidency "an interesting mix of brilliance and inadequacy." Casting about to explain how someone so "passive" in his management style could accomplish so much, Greenstein says that Reagan was in fact a "powerhouse . . . when he ha[d] a good team behind him."[69] The liberal historian Robert Dallek, critical of Reagan in several other respects, accords his economic policies "significant credit" for the "buoyant American economy of the 1980s and 1990s."[70] Harvard's Richard Neustadt admitted that Reagan had achieved something none of his seven predecessors had—he restored the public image of the office, making it "a place of popularity, influence, and initiative." After a generation or so, predicts Truman biographer Alonzo L. Hamby, Reagan will be "widely accepted by historians as a near-great chief executive."[71]

But popular historians such as Garry Wills and Haynes Johnson are dismissive of the man and the record. Reagan was a "kindly fanatic," concludes Wills, who could not distinguish between his film roles and reality. Thus Reagan got his idea for the SDI from his 1940 Brass Bancroft movie, *Murder in the Air,* which features an "inertia projector" that brings down enemy airplanes by knocking out their electrical systems.[72] For Johnson, Reagan is "the greatest mythmaker of all" whose domestic and foreign policies, far from creating national prosperity and leading to a peaceful end of the Cold War, left America debt-ridden and "more vulnerable" to the actions of terrorist Third World states.[73] Following Reagan's death, however, Johnson abandoned his thesis that the president had "sleep-walked" through history, but in fact had made history, saying, "His enduring legacy will be of the power of personality to uplift and transform the national spirit."[74] Wills also partially recanted his earlier summing up, at least in the field of foreign policy, writing that Reagan called the Soviet Union "an Evil Empire" and "it evaporated overnight."[75]

Despite his unequaled access to President Reagan, Edmund Morris found "Dutch" personally so inscrutable that he attempted to get at the "real" Reagan by pretending to have grown up with him—and even been rescued from drowning by him. Calling it a "new biographical style," Morris described pivotal events in Reagan's life as though he were personally present when in fact he was born several decades later and grew up thousands of miles away in Kenya and South Africa. Struggling to offer a summation, Morris described the perpetually sunny and engaging Reagan as an inexorable "glacier" about whom men will write, "How big he was! How far he came! And how deep the valley he carved!"[76] Casting about for presidential parallels, Morris suggested that Reagan would be remembered, along with Harry Truman and Andrew Jackson, as "one of the great populist presidents," revealing yet again the biographer's scant knowledge about American politics.[77]

The more apt comparison, as this biography has amply shown, would have been with Franklin Roosevelt and John Kennedy, both of whom understood and exercised an essential component of presidential power—the ability to persuade. But Reagan did not pander to the people—he always spoke from his own deep convictions that he believed the people shared. He was not being disingenuous in his farewell address when he said, "I wasn't a great communicator, but I communicated great things. And they didn't spring full blown from my brow, they came from the heart of a great nation—from our experience, our wisdom, and our belief in the principles that have guided us for two centuries."[78]

In the mass media, many commentators routinely refer to the 1980s as a decade of greed, talk about Reagan's habitual disengagement with critical affairs of state, equate the Iran-contra affair with Richard Nixon's truly scandalous Watergate, and credit everyone but Reagan with forging the Reagan Doctrine. Columnist Anthony Lewis of the *New York Times* dismissed Reagan's approach to foreign policy as "primitive" and "terribly dangerous." Reagan, he said, had a confrontational style based on the idea that "insult and intimidation were the keys to dealing successfully with the Soviet Union."[79] The Reagan years, wrote columnist Paul Krugman, were "a golden age for financial wheeling and dealing."[80]

The difficulty of many intellectuals to be objective about Reagan was underscored in the late fall of 2003 with the presentation of two television programs—*The Reagans* and *Angels in America*. The "biopic" about Ronald and Nancy Reagan was so cartoonish (the president as the near-sighted Mister Magoo and the first lady as Cruella DeVil) that an embarrassed CBS passed the program off to its pay-cable partner, Showtime. The initial manuscript of the three-hour film was riddled with startling inaccuracies such as the profoundly religious Reagan referring to himself as "the anti-Christ" and saying of AIDS, "They that live in sin shall die in sin." The truth of the matter is that President Reagan had declared—in April 1987—that AIDS was "public health enemy Number One."[81] "Ronald Reagan remains greatly loved for his service to his country and for the way he elevated American spirits during his two terms in office," wrote the *Washington Post*'s television critic Tom Shales. Why this film now? Shales asked, referring to Reagan's terminal Alzheimer's illness.[82] Despite its multiple distortions and misstatements, *The Reagans* received an Emmy nomination for best made-for-TV movie and nominations for best actor and best actress.

Tony Kushner's edgy, campy *Angels in America* is ostensibly about AIDS and homosexual life in America in the 1980s. But the central character of the six-hour "history" play, although he never appears, is Ronald Reagan, depicted by Kushner's characters as *the* symbol of "selfishness, greed, indifference to suffering, philosophical vacuity and saber-rattling patriotism." While Reagan did not cause AIDS, Kushner admitted, any public show of sympathy or concern by Reagan about the disease had to be muted in deference to an "unholy alliance" of fiscal conservatives and the religious Right. Kushner ignored that the federal government spent $5.727 billion on AIDS during the Reagan years, and that, for example, in his 1986 State of the Union Address, President Reagan mentioned AIDS five times.[83] As early as 1983, Margaret Heckler, Reagan's secretary of health and human services, declared that AIDS was her department's "number one priority."[84]

Like most Americans in the early and mid-1980s, Reagan did not recognize that AIDS was not just another disease like measles, which would in time "go away" (there were only 199 reported cases of AIDS in 1981). What changed the president's view, according to Lou Cannon, was the AIDS-related death in October 1985 of his longtime friend and sometime White House visitor—Hollywood film star Rock Hudson. While Reagan may not have done all that he could have done as the "great communicator" to educate the American public about AIDS, it is not accurate to trace his failure—as Kushner does—to the undue influence of the religious Right.

Like *The Reagans*, *Angels in America* was nominated for an Emmy and has become a basic source for many colleges and high schools. That is disturbing because for many young Americans, history is what Hollywood says it is.

I can personally attest to this fact of media-driven life. That same fall of 2003, while teaching a course on "The Politics of the Sixties" at the Catholic University of America, I came to the horrific events of November 22, 1963, and mentioned in passing how absurd were the conspiratorial theories of

Oliver Stone's *JFK* film, particularly the notion that Vice President Lyndon B. Johnson had been part of a plot to assassinate President John F. Kennedy. The face of my best student clouded over. What's wrong? I asked. "It's my favorite movie," she admitted. When almost every other student said that he or she had seen *JFK*, I responded, "Well, I can see we have a lot of unlearning to do." Even after a half hour of hard lecturing and extensive quotation from Gerald Posner's convincing study—*Case Closed*—I could sense that several students, including my straight A star, remained open to the suggestion that Johnson may have helped murder Kennedy. Such is the lasting influence of a critically acclaimed film.

We cannot concede the telling of history to the likes of Oliver Stone or Tony Kushner, especially the history of Ronald Reagan, who said in his farewell address, "We meant to change a nation, and instead we changed a world."[85] Was this a rare burst of grandiloquence from the usually modest Reagan, or an accurate summing up of a presidency? And did he change the nation and the world for better or for worse?

CHAPTER 8

Never Again

THERE IS NO DENYING, as the political scientist Andrew Busch states, that the Reagan years were marked by a high poverty rate, the loss of almost two million manufacturing jobs, a doubling of the national debt, scandals in and out of government, and an increase in terrorism. But President Reagan also revived a faltering economy, dispelled widespread public doubt about American ideals and institutions, and forged a foreign and national security policy that kept the peace and avoided war.[1] How did a man widely considered by many in the establishment to be too ancient, too ideological, and too detached restore Americans' confidence in themselves, set in motion an economic recovery that has persisted for almost two decades, and persuade Mikhail Gorbachev and the other *realpolitik* leaders of the Kremlin to end the Cold War at the bargaining table and not on the battlefield? Was it all just luck? Simply being in the right place at the right time? A correlation of objective forces?

Let us address the two most serious charges against Reagan and his presidency: one, the eighties were a decade of greed that benefited only the wealthy and neglected the middle class; and two, Reagan's dangerously belligerent foreign policy had little if anything to do with the disintegration of Soviet communism which was in an advanced state of decay and fated to collapse before long.

To begin with, President Reagan inherited the worst economy since the Great Depression. High tax rates were limiting jobs and investment, hurting the economy, and bringing in less than expected government revenue. The president reversed the process by reducing tax rates and government regulations that stabilized the economy and encouraged America's entrepreneurs. Taxes were cut across the board and not just for the wealthy. As a result, the share of federal income taxes paid by the top 1 percent rose from 18.1 percent in 1981 to 25 percent in 1990—a 28 percent increase—while the share of taxes paid by the bottom 50 percent fell from 7 percent to 6 percent—a 16 percent decrease. The number of Americans who had more than $1 million in assets increased from half a million to almost three times that many.[2]

With the Economic Recovery Tax Act of 1981, the Reagan administration set in motion forces which produced a sustained period of economic growth, starting in the fall of 1982 and lasting until now, that is unprecedented in U.S. history. Economist Paul Craig Roberts, who served as Reagan's first assistant secretary of the Treasury for economic policy, has estimated that from late 1982 through late 1987, unemployment fell an estimated 45 percent (down to 5.5 percent at the end of 1988), the consumer price index rose only 17 percent, private domestic investment grew 77 percent, the Dow Jones Industrial Average nearly tripled from 800 to 2,100, and economic growth averaged 4.6 percent annually—among the highest in the postwar period. The gross national product (GNP) nearly doubled. As a result, the real income of every strata of Americans increased, and total tax collections rose from $500 billion in 1980 to $1 trillion in 1990 (in constant dollars).[3]

So where did the $150 billion budget deficits come from? Roberts pointed out that the Reagan administration *never* forecast that the tax-rate reductions would "pay for themselves by recovering the lost revenues through higher economic growth." It predicted significantly higher government revenues but never a balanced budget. The ironic reason for the deficits is that inflation fell faster than predicted, wiping out $2.4 trillion in nominal GNP during 1982 to 1986—a dramatic reduction in the tax base. The budget deficits resulted because the supply-side policy "was more successful in reducing inflation" than the administration anticipated.[4] Supply-side economics was not a failure but just the opposite in its ability to stimulate growth and stifle inflation.

Conservative analyst David Frum has described the unbalanced budgets as "wartime deficits," saying that industrial nations typically run very large deficits during wartime. If the Reagan military buildup shortened and indeed ended the Cold War, as I and others have argued, then the budget deficits were a reasonable price to pay.[5]

At the same time, as analyst Lawrence Kudlow has stated, Reagan deregulated oil prices, making energy cheaper; launched U.S.-Canadian free trade, setting the stage for NAFTA (the North American Free Trade Agreement); and, perhaps most important of all, he created individual retirement accounts and 401(k) programs, giving birth to what Kudlow called "the investor class." Brand-new industries arose in computing, software, communications, and the Internet—"original endeavors that completely streamlined and transformed the American economy."[6]

President Reagan believed that low taxes and a solid dollar would generate economic growth with low inflation, and he helped to ensure the latter by naming Alan Greenspan chairman of the Federal Reserve. Despite two years of painful recession and low approval ratings at the beginning of his presidency, historian Michael Barone wrote, Reagan stayed the course and was "proven right." Few experts predicted in 1979 that America was about to enter nearly a quarter-century of low-inflation growth and that our economy would surge ahead of Europe's and Japan's. At the time, the academic journals were full of articles about the need for the United States to imitate "Japan, Inc." "Reagan did more than anyone else," Barone summed up, to make America's economic success happen.[7]

A Grand Strategy

How instrumental a role did Reagan play in the conduct of U.S. foreign policy in the 1980s and how critical was that policy in bringing about a peaceful end to the Cold War? Let's begin with the prepresidential years in the late 1970s when, according to presidential scholar Kiron Skinner, citizen Ronald Reagan formulated in his radio broadcasts and newspaper columns four core hypotheses about U.S.-Soviet relations and the Cold War.

First, Reagan argued that nuclear weapons "did not fundamentally change the nature of international relations." In his view, discussion of issues like Soviet expansionism had to precede any deliberations about arms control, not the reverse as had often been the case previously in the conduct of U.S. foreign policy. Second, Reagan believed that America was an "exceptional" nation in world history because it promoted freedom and equality at home and abroad. Such exceptionalism demanded that America match deeds with words in the promotion of freedom around the world. Third, Reagan saw the Soviet Union as an "abnormal" nation with no popular base of support, which suppressed freedom at home and abroad and was prepared to foment international crises as a means of maintaining its internal control. Fourth, Reagan asserted—and in the late 1970s it was his most contentious point—that the Soviet Union's inefficient economy and inferior technology "could not survive competition" with America.[8]

These ideas, discussed repeatedly by Reagan in his radio commentaries and newspaper columns from 1975 through 1979, constituted "a grand strategy" of peace through strength that he implemented as president. Rather than being a puppet at the end of someone's string, summarizes Skinner, "Reagan was a shrewd strategist who orchestrated events, wanted victory in the Cold War, and sensed that it was possible."[9]

Once elected and sworn in, Reagan proceeded with an across-the-board buildup of the defense establishment, which he found to be in a demoralized and weakened condition. According to Richard Perle, who served in Reagan's defense department, a third of the navy was unfit to sail, air-to-air munitions to Europe were "down to a four day supply," and it was uncertain whether NATO had the resolve to deploy medium-range missiles to counter new Soviet missiles aimed at Western Europe. But the morale of the American military soared as tens of billions of dollars were allotted for new land-based weapons, new ships, and new Cruise and other medium-range missiles. From inside the administration, Perle wrote, it was clear who was the architect of the strategy that in less than a decade ended the Cold War— "it was Reagan himself."[10]

The president set the new assertive tone in foreign policy at the very beginning of his administration. Ken Adelman, who was Reagan's director of the Arms Control and Disarmament Agency, recounts an early meeting of the National Security Council at which Secretary of State Alexander Haig brought up the Law of the Sea Treaty. While Haig admitted the treaty contained several provisions that the United States opposed, it had emerged from negotiations among 150 nations over a decade—therefore, we "had" to accept it. As Haig proceeded, at some length, to recite options for modifying the more objectionable parts of the treaty, a puzzled president finally interrupted. "Al," he asked, "isn't this what the whole thing was all about?" A mystified Haig asked the president what he meant.

Well, the president said, wasn't *not* going along with something that is "really stupid" just because 150 nations had done so what the whole thing—"our running, our winning, our governing"—was all about? A stunned Haig folded up his briefing book and promised to find out how to stop the treaty altogether. Ronald Reagan was "a leader of impressive skill and stunning vision," said Adelman, who worked closely with the president for most of the eighties.[11]

Many outside the administration and indeed outside U.S. borders agreed. Former Soviet dissident Natan Sharansky was in an eight-by-ten-foot cell in a Siberian prison in early 1983 when his Soviet jailers permitted him to read the latest copy of *Pravda,* the official communist newspaper. "Splashed across the front page," he recalled, was a condemnation of Ronald Reagan for calling the Soviet Union an "evil empire." Tapping on walls and talking through toilets, prisoners quickly spread the word of Reagan's "provocation." The dissidents were ecstatic. "Finally," Sharansky wrote, "the leader of the free world had spoken the truth—a truth that burned inside the heart of each and every one of us."[12] Lech Walesa, Nobel Peace prize winner and founder of the trade union Solidarity that confronted the communist regime, put it simply: "We in Poland . . . owe him our liberty."[13]

Conceding the importance of the U.S. military rearmament, the Strategic Defense Initiative, and the resistance to Soviet expansion in the Third World, Russian analyst Leon Aron stressed another Reagan initiative—in the realm of ideas. "Reagan did more than anyone [else]," he argued, "to delegitimate and demoralize the Soviet Union." The president—"sunny, serene, self-confident"—was not impressed by the Soviet Union's ten thousand nuclear missiles, its 5-million-strong army, or its annual production of more tanks than the rest of the world. For Reagan, said Aron, there was no parity, nuclear or otherwise, between America and the Soviet Union for one reason—the American people were free while the Soviet people were not. And he willingly shared his opinion with the entire world, stating matter-of-factly that the "evil empire" was headed for the "trash heap of history" [sic].[14] "There is little doubt," said the Russian expert, "that everything Reagan had said and done in [his first] four years was central to the almost palpable sense of foreboding and desperate need for change" which led in March 1985 to the nomination of Mikhail Gorbachev as general secretary of the Soviet Communist Party.[15] Barely six years later, Gorbachev, having no other choice, acceded to the dissolution of the Soviet Union and the interment of Soviet communism.

Reagan had his flaws of course and his administration made its share of mistakes, some of them serious. According to veteran biographer Lou Cannon, the president was slow to anger but very stubborn. He trusted "everyone who worked for him and considered even mild criticism" of his aides to be an attack on him or his policies. He once summarized his management philosophy as follows: "You surround yourself with the best people you can find, delegate authority, and don't interfere."[16] But what happens if the people are not all they should be and there are policy and jurisdictional conflicts that are not resolved? Things like Iran-contra happen. Nevertheless, Reagan survived Iran-contra (it will be no more than a historical footnote) because, as David Frum put it, the elements that were illegal—aiding anticommunist Nicaraguans—were popular and the elements that were unpopular—arming the "moderate" Iranians— were legal.[17]

Another decision that generated widespread and highly emotional criticism was Reagan's ceremonial visit in May 1985 to a German military cemetery in Bitburg, West Germany. The White House's vaunted advance team failed to notice that the cemetery contained the graves of some fifty Nazi SS troops. Protests poured in from the American Jewish community— Nobel laureate Elie Wiesel made a public plea to the president not to go to Bitburg. Veterans groups, Republican leaders, and Nancy Reagan all said that the visit would inflict needless damage on his presidency. But Reagan would not be moved. In his memoir, Reagan explained that once he had accepted the invitation from Chancellor Helmut Kohl, he could not embarrass him by canceling the visit. But beyond political embarrassment, Reagan said that it was not right "to keep on punishing every German for the Holocaust, including generations not yet born in the time of Hitler." "I have never regretted not canceling the trip to Bitburg," he wrote. "In the end, I believe my visit to the cemetery and the dramatic and unexpected gesture by two old soldiers from opposing sides of the battlefield [U.S. General Matthew Ridgway and German General Johannes Steinhoff] helped strengthen our European alliance and heal once and for all many of the lingering wounds of the war."[18]

The president rescued himself with a heart-felt eulogy to the Jewish victims of Nazism at the site of the infamous Bergen-Belsen concentration camp (whose most famous victim was Anne Frank) prior to his Bitburg visit. Saying that "no one of the rest of us can fully understand the enormity of the feelings carried by the victims of these camps," Reagan acknowledged the horror and brutality of Bergen-Belsen but then offered a hymn to the indomitable spirit of man:

> We are here to commemorate that life triumphed over the tragedy and the death of the Holocaust—overcame the suffering, the sickness, the testing, and, yes, the gassings.
>   Out of the ashes—hope, and from all the pain promise.[19]

Reagan was required to husband his resources in his second term as a result of serious surgeries—one in 1985 to remove cancerous polyps in his colon and another in early 1987 to remove his prostate. Each time he recovered in a remarkably short period of time for someone in his mid-70s. He also had to weather the shock of Nancy being diagnosed, in late 1987, with breast cancer; when she had a successful mastectomy, the president's natural buoyancy immediately returned. After his Alzheimer's became public in 1994, questions were raised whether Reagan had already started to have memory lapses while he was president, especially in the Iran-contra affair. Edmund Morris has provided a definitive answer, based on an essential fact: he remains the only person so far who has read all 500,000 words of Reagan's presidential dairy. The diary, all eight years of it, Morris wrote, "was uniform in style and cognitive content from beginning to end." There was "no hint of mental deterioration" beyond occasional repetitions and non sequiturs. If these are suggestions of early dementia, Morris said dismissively, "many diarists including myself would have reason to worry."[20]

Some writers, including Michael Deaver in his memoir, have emphasized Nancy's ability to sway Reagan, but most of the time the first lady did not "win" on key policy issues. For example, she lobbied the president to soften his rhetoric about the Soviet Union (he kept talking about the Evil Empire), to reduce military spending (he increased it), and not to push SDI at the expense of the disadvantaged (he retained SDI as the linchpin of his national security policy). She favored negotiation with the Sandinistas in Nicaragua—he chose to support the contras. And significantly, Nancy did not want her husband to run for reelection in 1984, concerned about the possibility of further attempts on his life. Instead, Reagan ran and won forty-nine states and 59 percent of the popular vote—achieving one of the most decisive victories in presidential politics.[21]

Nancy Reagan wielded the most decisive influence, and usually behind the scenes, in the area of personnel. When she felt that someone was not serving Reagan well or was putting his own interests ahead of the president's, she pushed, and hard, for his removal. She was, to use Lou Cannon's words, "the bad cop" who protected Reagan from "his own gullibility." It was Nancy who led the campaign for the removal of White House Chief of Staff Donald Regan, who badly mishandled the Iran-contra affair.[22]

It is often said that Reagan "rarely" initiated a meeting, a phone call, a proposal, or an idea. But this history shows that Reagan initiated the big ideas of his administration—strengthen America's defenses, lower everyone's taxes, appoint federal judges who would respect the Constitution, encourage free trade, end the Cold War by winning it. He then proceeded to exercise what Richard Neustadt calls "presidential power"—the ability to persuade the people that the policy he is proposing is in their best interest.[23] Reagan did not persuade the people in every instance—aid to the contras is one conspicuous failure—but he prevailed on such major issues as tax cuts, the military buildup, and free trade.

Reagan's first years of retirement in California were idyllic. He and Nancy moved into a handsome $2.5 million home in Bel Air, a few minutes from the president's office in Century City where he worked on his memoirs. He often escaped to his tiny mountaintop ranch near Santa Barbara to ride horses, trim trees, and do repairs on the house and grounds. In July 1989, he was thrown from his horse and suffered a massive brain contusion, but seemed to recover quickly following an operation. The following year, in September, the seventy-nine-year-old Reagan traveled to Berlin where, given a hammer and chisel, he carved several chunks out of the Wall. He then went to Gdansk, Poland, birthplace of the Solidarity movement, where Lech Walesa's former parish priest presented Reagan with a sword as thousands of Poles cheered. "I am giving you the saber," the priest said, "for helping us to chop off the head of communism."[24] Reagan stayed politically active, making twenty-nine personal or videotaped speeches for Republican candidates in 1990, and taping messages for conservative organizations such as Young America's Foundation.

However, at the Republican National Convention in the summer of 1992, he seemed initially hesitant in his remarks to the delegates but then hit his stride, receiving a standing ovation at the end. He was ready and willing to campaign for his former vice president that fall, but the Bush campaign asked him to do little. He did not say "I told you so," when Bill Clinton routed George H. W. Bush in California, which Reagan had carried ten times in primaries and general elections as governor and president.[25]

Now Nancy and their friends noted that the president was becoming more and more forgetful. On February 6, 1993, while celebrating his eighty-second birthday at the Reagan Presidential Library, Reagan delivered a graceful toast to his old friend Margaret Thatcher, and then repeated it word for word, leaving his audience embarrassed. His last major public appearance came at the funeral of Richard Nixon in April 1994, when much of the time he looked as though he did not know why he was there. Old friends continued to visit him in his Century City office, but there were no more public or political outings. At last, on his annual visit to the Mayo Clinic in the summer of 1994, Reagan's physicians confirmed what they had preliminarily diagnosed the year before—he was in the early stages of Alzheimer's.

The diagnosis led to his extraordinary two-page public letter in November 1994—"it had the simplicity of genius"—in which he disclosed he had Alzheimer's, and closed with these words to the American people he loved:

> Let me thank you . . . for giving me the great honor of allowing me to serve as your President. When the Lord calls me home, whenever that may be, I will leave with the greatest love for this country of ours and eternal optimism for its future.
>
> I now begin the journey that will lead me into the sunset of my life. I know that for America there will always be a bright dawn ahead.[26]

But Reagan could not resist making one last political gesture. Nine days later he wrote to the chairman of the Republican National Committee after Republicans led by Newt Gingrich had gained control of the U.S. House of Representatives for the first time in four decades: "I couldn't be happier with the results of the election. And please don't count me out! I'll be putting in my licks for Republicans as long as I'm able."[27]

What Makes a Leader?

The best of political leaders are not like you and me. Physically, they have remarkable vitality and stamina. They don't need energizer batteries to keep going and going through challenges and crises that would hospitalize many. Mentally, they are quick and facile, able to penetrate easily to the heart of an issue and to shift quickly from issue to issue. Philosophically, they have a set of core beliefs from which they rarely stray. They do not hesitate to go against the popular grain if they think it is in the best interests of the nation.

Such leaders embody the four essential qualities of leadership—courage, prudence, justice, and wisdom. Ronald Reagan had all four of these qualities and in abundance.

Courage

When he was shot on Monday afternoon, March 30, 1981, President seemed to spend most of his time reassuring everyone that he was not seriously hurt. As he was wheeled into the operating room, the president noted the long faces of his three top aides—James Baker, Ed Meese, Mike Deaver—standing in the hall and asked, "Who's minding the store?" Following the operation, Reagan scribbled a note to his doctors in the recovery room, "All in all, I'd rather be in Philadelphia."[28] Edmund Morris, winner of a Pulitzer Prize for his biography of Theodore Roosevelt, compared favorably the two presidents' reactions to attempted assassinations, concluding in a letter to the *New York Times* that "if our best and bravest continue to lead us, this Republic will somehow prevail."[29]

Reagan came by his sense of humor naturally. His father Jack Reagan was a gifted storyteller. His mother Nelle was well known for her public recitations and amateur acting. Reagan honed his skills in the commissary of Warner Brothers, where he sought out his Irish and Jewish colleagues and traded jokes and stories, sometimes for hours. Self-deprecating humor formed an essential part of Hollywood's culture. As president, Reagan "quipped, kidded, and bantered in nearly every White House meeting," putting aides and subordinates at ease and making them feel they were part of a historic enterprise. He also used humor, as Lincoln had, to express his fundamental ideas. For example, while Alan Greenspan and Martin Anderson in 1980 had constructed the budget rationale for Reagan's economic plan, it was Reagan who came up with the formulation that won the public's applause: "A recession is when your neighbor loses your job. A depression is when you lose yours. And recovery is when Jimmy Carter loses his."[30]

Reagan also used humor at his summit meetings with Mikhail Gorbachev as when he told the Soviet leader about the American and the Russian who were arguing about their two countries. The American said, "Look, I can go into the Oval Office, pound the president's desk, and say, 'Mr. President, I don't like the way you're running the country.' And the Russian responded, "I can do that too." The American said, "You can?" And the Russian responded, "Sure, I can go into the Kremlin, into the general secretary's office, and say, 'Mr. General Secretary, I don't like the way that President Reagan is running his country.'" Gorbachev laughed but got the point about the essential political difference between the two countries—a difference that Reagan emphasized in their discussions by quoting a Russian saying, "*Dovorey no provorey*" ("Trust, but verify").[31]

What would you and I do if we were diagnosed with Alzheimer's, that terrible thief of a disease that steals everything worth living for—your friends, your family, and finally yourself—and encases you in an empty shell of mind, body, and spirit? There would be denial, rage, endless speculation (why me?), and finally, perhaps, reluctant acceptance. As he did with every challenge in his life, Reagan confronted the reality of Alzheimer's, believing that even something that robbed him of everything was part of God's plan for him. Sitting at his desk in his California home, he told the world with a few strokes of his pen of his affliction. He said he hoped that his public letter would encourage "a clearer understanding" of Alzheimer's. He acknowledged the "heavy burden" his illness would impose on his beloved Nancy but expressed his conviction that she would face it with "faith and courage." And then he ended the letter, as he had ended his public addresses for decades, by thanking his "fellow Americans" and asking God to "always bless you."[32]

Reagan exhibited political courage upon taking office when he disregarded the conventional wisdom that counseled a tax increase and pushed hard for substantial tax cuts. There was strong opposition to SDI throughout the Reagan administration and at the highest levels. But Reagan did not budge, even at Reykjavik, sticking with SDI and thereby persuading the Soviets to stop waging an unwinnable Cold War.

Prudence

Rather than dispatching tens of thousands of troops around the world, President Reagan assisted pro-freedom anticommunist forces in carefully selected countries like Afghanistan, Nicaragua, Angola, and Cambodia. National security analyst Peter Schweizer estimates that the cash-strapped Soviets spent $8 billion a year on counterinsurgency operations against Reagan-backed guerrillas. The Soviets's military defeat in Afghanistan, for example, demoralized the Kremlin and the military.[33]

At home, Reagan practiced the politics of prudence by relying upon his "70 percent rule"—if he could get 70 percent of what he wanted, he would take his chances at getting the other 30 percent later. He wanted his 25 percent tax cut to take effect immediately in 1981 but reluctantly agreed to phase it in over three years. He accepted a deal with the Congressional Democrats in 1982 to raise more than $98.3 billion in additional taxes over three years in return for their agreement to cut spending by $280 billion during the same period. When the Democrats reneged on their promise, Reagan came back with the Tax Reform Act of 1986 that kept the economy growing and growing. "We got government out of the way," Reagan wrote, "and began the process of giving the economy back to the people."[34]

He also encouraged younger conservatives to continue the battle for limited government and individual freedom and responsibility. In 1986 a group of young activist Republicans led by Newt Gingrich (then a four-term Congressman from Georgia) called on the president to talk about the urgent need for new initiatives. Reagan listened patiently to their concerns and complaints for an hour. As he led them to the door, he said with a smile, "It took us seventy years to get into this mess, and I am going to lead the first eight years of getting out of it. Then, maybe you younger members will have to pick up and do some heavy lifting on your own after that." It was that challenge, recounts Gingrich, that led him and other Republican House members to welfare reform, a balanced budget, tax cuts, and other "Reaganite initiatives" in the 1994 Contract with America.[35]

Justice

Although it was not politically correct, President Reagan steadfastly defended the rights of every American from the moment of conception to that of natural death. For him the sanctity of life was not a slogan but a fundamental principle to be honored. He commented, to his former national security adviser William Clark and others, that his greatest regret as governor of California was signing a liberal abortion law. Reagan felt he had been "misled" about the impact of the legislation and opposed liberalized abortion at every future opportunity. When in 1983 he wrote "Abortion and the Conscience of the Nation" (an essay for *Human Life Review* later published as a short book), he became the first sitting president to write a book while in the White House. "The true question," Reagan often said, "is not when human life begins, but what is the true value and meaning of human life." He believed that the true answer to that question could only be found through faith and in prayer. He liked to quote Abraham Lincoln, who said, "I am frequently forced to my knees in the overwhelming conviction that I have no place else to go."[36]

Reagan insisted that his administration did not have separate social, economic, and foreign policy agendas but only one agenda, based on limited government, individual freedom and responsibility, peace through strength, and Judeo-Christian values. His administration sought not only to put America's financial house in order and rebuild the nation's defenses, but also to protect the unborn, end the manipulation of school children by utopian planners, and permit the acknowledgment of a supreme being in our classrooms. In his 1986 State of the Union address, Reagan said bluntly that there was "a wound in our national conscience; America will never be whole as long as the right to life granted by our Creator is denied to the unborn."[37] Colorado College professor Thomas Cronin, however, argued in the *New York Times* obituary of the president that he did not expand opportunities for "all Americans regardless of race, gender or income bracket."[38]

Such an assessment distorts badly the Reagan record. Black author, columnist and commentator Larry Elder has pointed out that during the eighties, black unemployment dropped 9 percentage points, black household income went up 84 percent, the number of black-owned businesses increased 40 percent, and receipts by black-owned businesses more than doubled, from $9.6 billion to $19.8 billion. Far from "torturing" blacks, as one black radio commentator alleged, Reagan treated them as he treated all Americans—as individuals with the ability to go as far as their talent and ambition would carry them.[39]

One astute observer, T. R. Reid of the *Washington Post*, said that the eighties were a period of creed, not greed, in which the number of Americans who volunteered their time for church, civic, and educational causes increased much faster than the population. On Main Street, if not Wall Street, the 1980s were a Me Decade.[40]

Wisdom

Reagan had the ability to see and foresee what others could not. While liberal intellectuals such as Arthur Schlesinger Jr. and John Kenneth Galbraith in the early eighties were lauding the economic accomplishments of the Soviet Union, Reagan told the British Parliament in the spring of 1982 that a "global campaign for freedom" would prevail over the forces of tyranny.[41] His prediction came true less than a decade later with the disintegration of the Soviet Union. A major reason for a peaceful end to the protracted conflict known as the Cold War was that Ronald Reagan perceived—when most conservatives and many liberals did not—that Mikhail Gorbachev was different from previous Soviet leaders. Gorbachev was, as Margaret Thatcher put it, a man that the West could do business with but on the condition stressed by Reagan—trust but verify.

In late 1981 and all of 1982 when his tax cuts had not yet kicked in and the U.S. economy still lagged, Reagan reassured his worried advisers and counseled them to stay the course. He had faith in the American people who if they could be "liberated from the restraints imposed on them by government" would pull "the country out of its tailspin."[42] In the closing days of 1982, America began the longest peacetime expansion in U.S. history, creating 17 million new jobs during the eighties and setting in motion a period of prosperity that continues to this day.

Another more prosaic quality made Reagan an extraordinary leader. He was a professional who studied hard at his profession, whether as sports announcer, film actor, public speaker, political candidate, governor, or president. He prepared himself for every occasion, from the Drake Relays to *King's Row* to "A Time for Choosing" to a debate with Jimmy Carter to a summit with Mikhail Gorbachev to a State of the Union address. He was a natural communicator as Ted Williams was a natural hitter and Luciano Pavarotti was a natural singer, but like them, he did not leave things to chance. An aid of long standing was a packet of about one hundred index cards, four inches by six inches, on which Reagan had written in hand his favorite quotations. The cards contained 339 quotations from the writings of a remarkably varied group, including Aristotle, Abraham Lincoln, Theodore and Franklin Roosevelt, Lenin and Stalin, Lord Acton, James Madison, Frederic Bastiat, Confucius and Pericles, the Bible and Cicero. In his 1984 presidential debate with Walter Mondale, when Reagan was asked whether he thought he would be able to "function" given that he was the oldest president in history, Reagan's answer included this Cicero quotation: "Had there not been older men to undo the damage done by the young, there would be no state."[43]

He was, wrote Peter J. Wallison, who served as counsel to the president, "the very embodiment of the best in the people who elected him twice to the country's highest office."[44] Summing him up, the political philosopher Michael Novak said that Reagan "awoke the better angels of our nature."[45] Ronald Reagan's trust in the people and his love of freedom were rooted in two essential American documents—the Declaration of Independence and the Constitution. From his very first national speech on behalf of Barry

Goldwater's presidential bid in October 1964 to his farewell address to the nation in January 1989, Reagan turned again and again to the wisdom and the philosophy of the Founders. Indeed, more than once, he sounded like one of them.

In his televised address for Goldwater, Reagan declared that the idea "that government is beholden to the people, that it has no other source of power except the sovereign people, is still the newest and most unique idea in all the long history of man's relation to man." In his farewell address as president, Reagan reiterated the central role of the American Revolution in our history. He said: "Ours was the first revolution in the history of mankind that truly reversed the course of government, and with three little words: "'We the people.'" "'We the people,'" he said, "tell the government what to do, it doesn't tell us." The idea of "we the people," he explained, was the underlying basis for everything he had tried to do as president.[46]

Confirmation of Reagan's deep respect for the founding came from political scientist Matthew J. Franck, who estimated that Reagan talked more about the Founders than any president "in living memory." Indeed, Reagan mentioned the "Framers" or the "Founding Fathers" more often than all of his nine predecessors combined.[47] His favorite founders were Thomas Jefferson and Thomas Paine.

President Reagan ended his farewell address—it was his thirty-fourth talk from the Oval Office—by referring to America as the "shining city on a hill," a phrase he had borrowed from the Pilgrim leader John Winthrop and modified, adding the word "shining." The implicit reference to that first city on a hill—Jerusalem—was clear to Winthrop and his followers and to Reagan as well.

The president asked the millions watching him on television that cold January evening:

And how stands the city on this winter night? . . . after two hundred years, two centuries, she still stands strong and true on the granite edge, and her glow has held steady no matter what storm. And she's still a beacon, still a magnet, for all who must have freedom, for all the pilgrims from all the lost places who are hurtling through the darkness, toward home.

He reassured the men and women of the "Reagan revolution" that they had made a difference—they had made the city stronger and freer and had left her in good hands. "All in all," he concluded, with just the suggestion of a twinkle in his eye, "not bad, not bad at all."[48]

And then, having survived an assassin's bullet, two cancer operations, an elongated recession, the slings and arrows of outraged liberals about his tax cuts, the alarums of nervous conservatives about his summit meetings with Gorbachev, a 35 percent approval rating, the Iran-contra scandal and the Bitburg controversy, the self-serving memoirs of David Stockman and Donald Regan, a Democratic majority in the House and the loss of a GOP majority in the Senate, the "borking" of Supreme Court justice nominee Robert Bork and the frequent savaging of his beloved Nancy , having done his duty and served his country as few presidents have in our history, Ronald Reagan went home.

Bibliographic Essay

Even before Ronald Reagan's death in June 2004, there were several thousand books about the former president available through Amazon.com, including works by former presidential aides, cabinet members, ambassadors, journalists, historians, and members of his family. That number is certain to increase in the years to come as analysts and academics explore Reagan's career and attempt to assess his place among American presidents and in our nation's history.

I found the following works to be essential for a proper understanding of our fortieth president: *Reagan in His Own Hand* and *Reagan: A Life in Letters*, both edited by Kiron Skinner, Annelise Anderson, and Martin Anderson. The former is a collection of nearly seven hundred radio manuscripts that Reagan researched and wrote in the mid-1970s. Their breadth and depth are remarkable, covering nearly every domestic and foreign policy issue and leading the editors to describe Reagan as "a one-man think tank." Contained in these commentaries are most of the major themes of his presidency—the urgent need to trim the size of government and contest the imperial ambitions of the Soviet Union. If you would know a public man, it has been said, read his private letters. Reagan may have written as many ten thousand letters in his lifetime, making him the most prolific writer of all our presidents. The letters cover an amazing variety of subjects—from SDI to the kind of hearing aid he wore—and are addressed to the famous and the unknown, to old friends from his childhood and to ordinary citizens concerned about the economy and nuclear war. Here in his own words is the unabridged Ronald Reagan.

Where's the Rest of Me? and *An American Life*, both by Ronald Reagan. The first book—in which Reagan is often eloquent and rarely boring—was written with Richard G. Hubler and published in 1965 just before Reagan declared himself a candidate for governor of California. Many writers have dismissed it as unimportant—Edmund Morris called it "pedantic"—but I believe it reveals how Reagan evolved from a liberal Democrat in the thirties into a conservative Republican in the fifties. An appendix includes the text of the 1964 speech that made Reagan a national political star—"A Time for Choosing." Most presidential biographies are dull and predictable—Ulysses S. Grant's memoir is an exception—but *An American Life* does allow us to watch Reagan—often through excerpts from his daily diary—as he wrestles with prickly problems such as the trip to Bitburg, West Germany, and the Iran-contra affair.

Angels Don't Die: My Father's Gift of Faith by Patti Davis and *The City on a Hill* by Michael Reagan. Patti Davis, the once estranged but now reconciled daughter of Ron and Nancy Reagan, offers a moving tribute to her father's spiritual strength that enabled him to weather crises and challenges throughout his life. Davis thanks her father-president for giving her a "legacy of faith." Michael Reagan followed his father into radio to become the host of a top-rated talk show and is, with the death of his older sister Maureen, the most conservative of the three Reagan children. He provides a blueprint for rebuilding the "shining city on a hill" to which his father so often referred, starting with a proper balance among the four essential elements of a healthy society—government, business, religious-civic, and family. A special feature of the book are the many telling stories that Michael recounts about his father.

President Reagan: The Role of a Lifetime and *Governor Reagan: His Rise to Power*, both by Lou Cannon, the former *Washington Post* reporter who covered Reagan during his gubernatorial and presidential years. His obituary in the *Post* is an excellent summary of Reagan's life and career and far superior to that of Marilyn Berger in the *New York Times*. Inclined to stress the actor side of Reagan in his early writing, Cannon increasingly emphasized Reagan's political and analytical skills in the later editions of his biographies. Cannon is usually fair in his judgments and always reliable as to the facts.

With Reagan: The Inside Story by Edwin Meese III, *Revolution* by Martin Anderson, *When Character Was King* by Peggy Noonan, and *Nofziger* by Lyn Nofziger. These are the most insightful memoirs by four people who worked closely with Reagan in a variety of posts. Meese was next to Reagan throughout his years of public service, first as chief of staff to Governor Reagan and then as counselor to the president and attorney general. When he says Reagan believed this or said that, you can be certain he did. Anderson was Reagan's chief domestic and economic policy adviser from 1981 to 1982 and gives an insider's view of supply-side economics as well as the 1980 presidential campaign that put Reagan in the White House. Noonan drafted some of Reagan's most memorable speeches (including his comments on the "Challenger" disaster), and her recollections about Reagan's deep involvement in the speech-writing process are interesting. But the real value of her book is the intuitive analysis of Reagan's character. His two greatest traits, she writes, were courage and tenacity. Nofziger is a political journalist turned political adviser noted for his irreverent attitude about nearly everything, including the politicians he worked for. A self-proclaimed conservative, he was Reagan's press secretary in his 1966 gubernatorial campaign and wound up in the Reagan White House. Nofziger captures the special relationship between Ron and Nancy Reagan, who he says is more responsible than any other person for the president's political success.

Reagan's War: The Epic Story of His Forty-Year Struggle and Final Triumph over Communism by Peter Schweizer; *Turmoil and Triumph: My Years as Secretary of State* by George Shultz, and *Fighting for Peace: Seven Critical Years in the Pentagon* by Caspar W. Weinberger. Taken together, these books by a knowledgeable outsider (Schweizer) and two powerful cabinet secretaries (Shultz and Weinberger) provide a comprehensive picture of Reagan's foreign and national security policy. Schweizer details Reagan's economic and political war against the Soviet Union, drawing upon heretofore closed files. Shultz and Weinberger document that Reagan was a hands-on chief executive when the issue was one he deemed crucial—like SDI or the negotiations with Mikhail Gorbachev.

Useful to an understanding of Reagan are *Ronald Reagan: How an Ordinary Man Became an Extraordinary Leader* by Dinesh D'Souza, and *How Ronald Reagan Changed My Life* by Peter Robinson. D'Souza, who worked briefly in the White House as a domestic policy adviser, is best at summing up Reagan's personal strengths—such as his conviction that he could handle the complex issues of the presidency far better than his critics realized. Robinson joined the Reagan speechwriting team as a young man and stayed for six years. His account of the "Mr. Gorbachev, tear down this Wall!" speech is a classic Washington tale. The bureaucrats in the State Department and the National Security Council kept removing the exhortation, and President Reagan kept putting it back in. But it is the personal side rather than the policy side of the book that is the most affecting. Robinson describes how Reagan molded his life, especially through "a certain lightness of touch."

Dutch by Edmund Morris is the most disappointing of all the books about Ronald Reagan. The author is an enormously gifted writer and prize-winning biographer who had unrestricted access to President Reagan throughout his second term and beyond and who after fourteen years published a bizarre book filled with made-up characters, quotations, and footnotes. In an attempt to write about someone whom he found impenetrable, like a piece of granite or a glacier, Morris pretends in the early chapters to be a contemporary of Reagan in Dixon and Hollywood. This literary technique allows him to offer fictional observations about the actor and emerging politician derived, the author insists, from Reagan's way of looking at life. But who can tell what is fact and what is fiction, what is Morris and what is Reagan, in the midst of all the invented people, conversations, and letters? Morris could have written another prize-winning biography about one of the most consequential presidents of the twentieth century. Instead he produced a book that provides the occasional acute observation—such as his dismissal of the suggestion that Reagan suffered from Alzheimer's during his presidency—but is destined to be only a footnote in the vast literature about the fortieth president.

Among the collections of academic essays that offer a balanced evaluation of Reagan's legacy are *The Reagan Presidency: Pragmatic Conservatism and Its Legacies*, edited by W. Elliot Brownlee and Hugh Davis Graham, which presents itself as a "second generation" evaluation of the so-called Reagan Revolution. Academics James T. Patterson and Beth Fischer dispute any notion of "revolution" and describe President Reagan as reactive and middle of the road rather than revolutionary. However, most of the contributors to *The Reagan Presidency* find that Reagan was successful in carrying out his core agenda and see significant long-term effects on conservative politics and policymaking. Another balanced book is *The Reagan Record*, edited by John L. Palmer and Isabel V. Sawhill, who say that the Reagan administration was "revolutionary in purpose but evolutionary in practice." Achievements included staying the course on tax cuts, keeping the social safety net intact along with tough new workfare programs, and producing the lowest rate of inflation in many years. The

Reagan administration, they say, implemented a "substantial shift" in national priorities and sparked a "fresh debate" about the purposes of government.

Far more critical of the Reagan presidency and more typical of the academic literature are *The Economy in the Reagan Years: The Economic Consequences of the Reagan Administration* by Anthony S. Campagna; *The Reagan Effect: Economic and Presidential Leadership* by John W. Sloan; *Assessing the Reagan Years* edited by David Boaz; and *The Reagan Paradox: U.S. Foreign Policy in the 1980s* by Coral Bell. Campagna says flatly that the economic program of the Reagan years failed, leaving the economy with "many more serious problems to solve" than if this "unwarranted and deceptive program had not been adopted." While willing to concede the long-term influence of the Reagan tax cuts, Sloan states that what he calls Reagan's "visions" contributed to budget deficits, trade deficits, and the "savings and loan debacle." The Cato Institute's David Boaz assembled a group of libertarian analysts who conclude that the Reagan Revolution "turned out to be a paper tiger"—federal spending kept rising and federal regulations kept increasing. Reagan did change the tone of debate about the role of government, Boaz and his colleagues concede, but they add that it is doubtful the achievement will endure. Australian professor Bell writes that although Reagan's foreign policy rhetoric was initially simplistic and "Rambo-like," what he accomplished in places like China and Central America showed "a great continuity" with past policies. She cites the paradox between hard words and relatively soft deeds and concludes that a good many of the Reagan-era policies were really "smoke and mirrors."

In a category by itself is *The Reagan Legacy*, edited by *Washington Post* reporters Sidney Blumenthal and Thomas Byrne Edsall, who point out that five of their seven contributors conclude that the Reagan Revolution was a failure. Two examples are the nonrestoration of American influence and prestige around the world and the undermining of the rule of law at home. Coeditor Edsall, however, avers that the Reagan presidency produced a "major alteration" of the nation's political and economic structure. All the authors agree that President Reagan did change the terms of the national political debate.

Finally, I list *The Age of Reagan: The Fall of the Old Liberal Order 1964–1980* by Steven F. Hayward; *Ronald Reagan and the Politics of Freedom* by Andrew E. Busch; *God and Ronald Reagan* by Paul Kengor;

and *The Right Moment: Ronald Reagan's First Victory and the Decisive Turning Point in American Politics* by Matthew Dallek. These books by four brilliant young scholars describe the political times in which Reagan came to power; Reagan's political philosophy, solidly based on the American founding; his deeply rooted Christian faith; and his amazingly successful entry into politics in 1966. Hayward is especially good at detailing the reasons for the fall of the old liberal order. He, Busch, Kengor, and Dallek are in the first wave of younger political scientists and historians who do not have the ideological hang-ups of an older generation and will be able to offer a more objective portrait of Ronald Reagan and his presidency.

Acknowledgments

RONALD REAGAN HAS BEEN A FAVORITE SUBJECT OF MINE for nearly forty years, beginning in 1965 when I traveled with him in California as he was considering a new career in politics. I knew from the beginning that he was a special kind of politician and would go far, even as far as the White House. In 1967, I wrote the first political biography of him (which I revised and updated in 1980 and then in 1981). I devoted two chapters to his presidency in *The Conservative Revolution* (Free Press, 1999), my political history of the modern American conservative movement. I have also written dozens of articles and op-ed articles about Reagan, lectured about him at many venues here in America and overseas, and have been interviewed on most major television and radio programs about him (particularly in the week following his death). I have drawn upon all of these sources for this biography as well as the ever-increasing flow of books and information about our fortieth president.

A number of research assistants have helped me over the years, the most recent and one of the very best being Matthew Sitman. I wish to thank my literary agent Leona Schecter for her continuing professional guidance, Washington editor Christopher Anzalone of Rowman & Littlefield for his encouragement, and Dr. Edwin J. Feulner of the Heritage Foundation for his and the Foundation's invaluable support of my research and writing. And I acknowledge the indispensable help of the indispensable person in my life—my wife Anne.

Lee Edwards
July 2004

Notes

Preface

1. From remarks by Ronald Reagan to the nation on the *Challenger* disaster, January 28, 1986, *Speaking My Mind,* Ronald Reagan, New York, 1989: 292. Taken from a poem by the American pilot John Gillespie Magee Jr., who died in December 1941 on a routine training mission.
2. Audrey Hudson and Stephen Dinan, "Popular Leader's Passing Sad Day," *Washington Times*, June 6, 2004.
3. Ibid.
4. "Ronald Wilson Reagan 1911–2004," *Washington Times,* June 6, 2004.
5. "A Robust Economy, a Soaring National Debt," Owen Ullmann, *USA Today*, June 7, 2004.
6. Marilyn Berger, "Ronald Reagan Dies at 93: Fostered Cold-War Might and Curbs on Government," *New York Times*, June 6, 2004.
7. Ibid.
8. Ibid.
9. Steve Miller, "Reagan Critics Decry Glowing Tributes," *Washington Times*, June 8, 2004.
10. Bill Plante, June 7, 2004, *CBS Evening News*; Peter Jennings, June 10, 2004, ABC's *Good Morning America*; Morley Safer, June 14, 2004, CNN's *Larry King Live*, as reported in *Notable Quotables*, June 21, 2004, vol. 17, no. 13, Media Research Center.
11. "Reagan Remembered as Spirit of America," *USA Today*, June 7, 2004.
12. "Ronald Wilson Reagan," an editorial, *Washington Times*, June 6, 2004.
13. David Ignatius, "Protean Leader," *Washington Post*, June 8, 2004.

14. David Von Drehle, "Ronald Reagan Dies; 40th President Reshaped American Politics," *Washington Post*, June 6, 2004.
15. Michael Beschloss, "The Thawing of the Cold War," *Newsweek*, June 14, 2004: 41.
16. Lou Cannon, "Why Reagan Was the 'Great Communicator,'" *USA Today*, June 7, 2004.
17. David Brooks, " Reagan's Promised Land," *New York Times*, June 8, 2004; Martin Kasindorf, "A Nation Remembers: The Life and Legacy of Ronald Wilson Reagan," *USA Today*, June 7, 2004.
18. Debbie Howlett, "'Standards and Values' Developed in Small Town; Boyhood Home of Dixon, Ill., Had Lasting Influence," *USA Today*, June 8, 2004; James G. Lakely, "'God's Plan' Guided Reagan's Life," *Washington Times*, June 7, 2004.
19. "Remembering Ronald Reagan: The Funeral and Burial," *Washington Post*, June 12, 2004.
20. "Eulogizing Reagan," *Washington Times*, June 7, 2004.
21. S. A. Miller, "Mourn," *Washington Times*, June 10, 2004.
22. Sue Anne Pressley, "Thousands Come to Witness History, Pay Their Respects," *Washington Post*, June 10, 2004.
23. Joel Achenbach, "An American Journey," *Washington Post*, June 10, 2004.
24. Rene Sanchez, "The Last Ride Home," *Washington Post*, June 12, 2004.
25. Michael Barone, "He Leaves a Surprisingly Grand Legacy," *U.S. News & World Report*, June 2004: 78.

Introduction

1. Lyn Nofziger, *Nofziger,* Washington, D.C., 1992: 179.
2. Lee Edwards, *The Conservative Revolution: The Movement That Remade America,* New York, 1999; also Peggy Noonan, *When Character Was King: A Story of Ronald Reagan*, New York, 2001: 202.
3. Nofziger, *Nofziger*: 178.
4. Ibid.
5. Steven Hayward, *The Age of Reagan: The Fall of the Old Liberal Order 1964–1980*, New York, 2001: 438.
6. "Reagan's 'Gloves-Off' Campaign Successful," *Human Events*, April 3, 1976: 4.

7. M. Stanton Evans, interview with the author, May 10, 1996.
8. "My First 100 Days," An Interview with Ronald Reagan, *Conservative Digest,* August 1976: 6.
9. Joseph Lelyveld, "The Importance of a TV Speech," *Washington Star,* March 29, 1976.

Chapter 1

1. Anne Edwards, *Early Reagan*, New York, 1987: 35.
2. Lee Edwards, *Ronald Reagan: A Political Biography,* Houston, Texas, 1981: 19.
3. Lou Cannon, *President Reagan: The Role of a Lifetime*, New York, 2000: 177.
4. Ronald Reagan with Richard G. Hubler, *Where's the Rest of Me?* New York, 1965: 8.
5. Cannon, *President Reagan*: 176.
6. Reagan, *Where's the Rest of Me?* 8.
7. Bill Boyarsky, *The Rise of Ronald Reagan*, New York, 1968: 39.
8. Anne Edwards, *Early Reagan*: 40.
9. Cited by Helene von Damm, *Sincerely, Ronald Reagan*, New York, 1980: 91.
10. Ibid.
11. Paul Kengor, *God and Ronald Reagan: A Spiritual Life*, New York, 2004: 11–12.
12. Lee Edwards, *Ronald Reagan*: 21.
13. Remarks of President Reagan at the annual National Prayer Breakfast, February 4, 1982.
14. Samuel Eliot Morison, *The Oxford History of the American People,* vol. 3, New York, 1972: 220.
15. Reagan, *Where's the Rest of Me?*: 18.
16. Ronald Reagan to Helen P. Miller, September 3, 1981, as reprinted in *Reagan: A Life in Letters*, ed. Kiron K. Skinner, Annelise Anderson, Martin Anderson, New York, 2003: 7–8.
17. Edmund Morris, *Dutch: A Memoir of Ronald Reagan*, New York, 1999: 40.
18. Kengor, *God and Ronald Reagan*: 24–25.
19. Morris, *Dutch*: 42.
20. *Reagan: A Life in Letters*: 9–10.
21. Reagan, *Where's the Rest of Me?*: 17.

22. Anne Edwards, *Early Reagan*: 43.
23. Kengor, *God and Ronald Reagan*: 30.
24. Lee Edwards, *Reagan*: 22; Boyarsky, *The Rise of Ronald Reagan*: 36.
25. Dinesh D'Souza, *Ronald Reagan*, New York, 1997: 40.
26. Morris, *Dutch*: 54.
27. Ibid.
28. Ibid.
29. Morison, *The Oxford History of the American People, volume 3*: 281.
30. Anne Edwards, *Early Reagan*: 73.
31. Ronald Reagan to Leonard Kirk, March 23, 1983, *Reagan: A Life in Letters*: 13.
32. Kengor, *God and Ronald Reagan*: 42.
33. Reagan, *Where's the Rest of Me?*: 26.
34. Ibid.: 28–29.
35. Ibid.
36. See Lou Cannon, *Governor Reagan: His Rise to Power*, New York, 2003: 26–27.
37. Cannon, *Governor Reagan*: 34.
38. Lee Edwards, *Reagan*: 28.
39. Ibid.
40. Morris, *Dutch*: 703.
41. Reagan, *Where's the Rest of Me?*: 43.
42. Lee Edwards, *Reagan*: 29.
43. Morison, *The Oxford History of the American People, vol. 3*: 290.
44. Reagan, *Where's the Rest of Me?*: 45.
45. Ibid.: 44.

Chapter 2

1. Lee Edwards, *Reagan*: 31.
2. Reagan, *Where's the Rest of Me?*: 49–50.
3. Cannon, *Governor Reagan*: 38.
4. Roger Rosenblatt, with Laurence I. Barrett, "Out of the Past, Fresh Choices for the Future," *Time*, January 5, 1981: 13–14.
5. Cannon, *President Reagan*: 187.
6. Lee Edwards, *Reagan*: 35.
7. Anne Edwards, *Early Reagan*: 143.
8. Quoted in George F. Will, *The Woven Figure: Conservatism and America's Fabric*, New York, 1997: 108.

9. Morris, *Dutch*: 132.
10. Reagan, *Where's the Rest of Me?*: 53.
11. Anne Edwards, *Early Reagan*: 150.
12. William Manchester, *The Glory and the Dream: A Narrative History of America 1932–1972, vol. 1*, Boston, 1973: 171.
13. Reagan, *Where's the Rest of Me?*: 72; Anne Edwards, *Early Reagan*: 154.
14. Reagan, *Where's the Rest of Me?*: 74.
15. Ibid.
16. Morris, *Dutch*: 157.
17. Reagan, *Where's the Rest of Me?*: 76.
18. Anne Edwards, *Early Reagan*: 163.
19. Ibid.: 172.
20. Ibid.: 178.
21. Reagan, *Where's the Rest of Me?*: 81.
22. D'Souza, *Ronald Reagan*: 45.
23. Reagan, *Where's the Rest of Me?*: 92.
24. Anne Edwards, *Early Reagan*: 214.
25. Reagan, *Where's the Rest of Me?*: 95.
26. Anne Edwards, *Early Reagan*: 193.
27. Kengor, *God and Ronald Reagan*: 49.
28. Ibid.
29. Reagan, *Where's the Rest of Me?*: 5–6; Boyarsky, *The Rise of Ronald Reagan*: 67.
30. Reagan, *Where's the Rest of Me?*: 6–7.
31. Anne Edwards, *Early Reagan*: 228.
32. Ibid.: 229.
33. Ibid.: 231.
34. Manchester, *The Glory and the Dream*: 279; Reagan, *Where's the Rest of Me?*: 99.
35. Morris, *Dutch*: 12.
36. Anne Edwards, *Early Reagan*: 231.
37. Reagan, *Where's the Rest of Me?*: 107.
38. Anne Edwards, *Early Reagan*: 273; Reagan, *Where's the Rest of Me?*: 117.
39. *Reagan: A Life in Letters*: 132.
40. Ibid.: 118.
41. Reagan, *Where's the Rest of Me?*: 118.
42. Ibid.: 120.

43. Ibid.: 124.
44. Ibid.: 125.

Chapter 3

1. Reagan, *Where's the Rest of Me?*: 139, 141.
2. Lee Edwards, *Ronald Reagan*: 52.
3. Reagan, *Where's the Rest of Me?*: 164–65.
4. From an interview with George Murphy in March 1967 and cited in Lee Edwards, *Ronald Reagan*: 53.
5. Ibid.
6. Ibid.: 54.
7. *Reagan: A Life in Letters*: 148.
8. Ibid.: 55.
9. Edmund Morris, *Dutch*: 257; Hedda Hopper, "Mr. Reagan Airs His Views," *Chicago Tribune*, May 18, 1947.
10. Anne Edwards, *Early Reagan*: 348.
11. *Reagan: A Life in Letters*: 149.
12. Lee Edwards, *Ronald Reagan*: 57.
13. Anne Edwards, *Early Reagan*: 355.
14. Ibid.: 355.
15. Ibid.: 382–87.
16. Lee Edwards, *Ronald Reagan*: 58.
17. Ibid.: 58.
18. Cannon, *Governor Reagan*: 78.
19. Reagan, *An American Life*: 123.
20. Ibid.: 59.
21. Based on a conversation with Edwin Meese III, August 8, 2003.
22. Anne Edwards, *Early Reagan*: 441.
23. Matthew Dallek, *The Right Moment: Ronald Reagan's First Victory and the Decisive Turning Point in American Politics*, New York, 2000: 32.
24. Ibid.: 294.
25. Lee Edwards, *Ronald Reagan*: 67.
26. Anne Edwards, *Early Reagan*: 404.
27. Cannon, *President Reagan*: 246.
28. Kengor, *God and Ronald Reagan*: 95.
29. Morris, *Dutch*: 292.
30. Anne Edwards, *Early Reagan*: 444.

31. Dallek, *The Right Moment*: 37.
32. Lee Edwards, *Ronald Reagan*: 62.
33. Reagan: *Where's the Rest of Me?*: 266.
34. Anne Edwards, *Early Reagan*: 454.
35. Lee Edwards, *Ronald Reagan*: 63.
36. Anne Edwards, *Early Reagan*: 455.
37. Lee Edwards, *Ronald Reagan*: 63.
38. Ibid.: 64.
39. Ibid.
40. Anne Edwards, *Early Reagan*: 466.
41. Reagan, *Where's the Rest of Me?*: 268–71.
42. Morris, *Dutch*: 314.
43. Lee Edwards, *Ronald Reagan*: 65.
44. Anne Edwards, *Early Reagan*: 457.
45. Morris, *Dutch*: 309; Reagan, *Where's the Rest of Me?*: 297.
46. Dallek, *The Right Moment*: 38.
47. Lee Edwards, *Ronald Reagan*: 67.
48. Reagan, *Where's the Rest of Me?*: 297.
49. Ronald Reagan, *An American Life*, New York, 1990: 140; Lee Edwards, *Goldwater: The Man Who Made a Revolution*, Washington, D.C., 1995: 334.
50. Reagan, *An American Life*; 140–41.
51. "A Time for Choosing," a televised national address on behalf of Senator Barry Goldwater, October 27, 1964, as reprinted in Ronald Reagan, *Speaking My Mind*, New York, 1989: 24–36.
52. "Ronald Reagan and the American Public Philosophy," a paper presented to the Conference on the Reagan presidency at the University of California, Santa Barbara, May 27–30, 2002, by Hugh Heclo, Robinson Professor of Public Affairs, George Mason University: 4–5.
53. "A Time for Choosing," op. cit.
54. Stephen Hess and David Broder, *The Republican Establishment: The Present and the Future of the G.O.P.*, New York, 1967: 254.
55. Author's interview with Henry Salvatori, December 21, 1991.

Chapter 4

1. Lee Edwards, *Ronald Reagan*: 75.
2. Reagan, *An American Life*: 145.

3. Lee Edwards, *Ronald Reagan*: 76.
4. Boyarsky, *The Rise of Ronald Reagan*: 143.
5. Author's interview with Ronald Reagan, October 13–14, 1965, Los Angeles, California.
6. Ibid.
7. Ibid.
8. Cannon, *Governor Reagan*: 139.
9. Reagan, *An American Life*: 147.
10. Lawrence E. Davies, "Reagan Assesses Political Future," *New York Times*, July 25, 1965.
11. Lee Edwards, *Ronald Reagan*: 104.
12. Ibid.
13. Ibid.: 98–99.
14. Lee Edwards, *The Conservative Revolution*: 157–58.
15. Cannon, *Governor Reagan*: 143.
16. Ibid.: 107.
17. Ibid.: 106.
18. Fawn M. Brodie, "Ronald Reagan Plays Surgeon," *The Reporter*, April 6, 1967: 11; Cannon, *President Reagan*: 108–9
19. Cannon, *President Reagan*: 116.
20. Lee Edwards, *Goldwater*: 90.
21. Dallek, *The Right Moment*: 124–25.
22. Lee Edwards, *Ronald Reagan*: 87.
23. Dallek, *The Right Moment*: 175.
24. Lee Edwards, *Ronald Reagan*: 133; Cannon, *President Reagan*: 117.
25. Dallek, *The Right Moment*: 241.
26. Lee Edwards, *Ronald Reagan*: 158.
27. Gary G. Hamilton and Nicole Woolsey Biggart, *Governor Reagan, Governor Brown: A Sociology of Executive Power*, New York, 1984: 184–85. Edwin Meese III told me (in August 2003) that the memorandum accurately reflects Ronald Reagan's political philosophy.
28. Hamilton and Biggart, *Governor Reagan, Governor Brown: A Sociology of Executive Power*: 165.
29. "Reagan's Real Record in California," *U.S. News & World Report*, February 9, 1976: 15.
30. Hamilton and Biggart, *Governor Reagan, Governor Brown*: 166.
31. Ibid.

32. Caspar W. Weinberger, "A Most Remarkable President," *Libertas,* July 2004: 4. Published by Young America's Foundation.
33. Lee Edwards, *Ronald Reagan*: 162.
34. D'Souza, *Ronald Reagan*: 65.
35. Cannon, *Governor Reagan*: 227.
36. Lee Edwards, *Ronald Reagan*: 164.
37. Boyarsky, *The Rise of Ronald Reagan*: 189.
38. Cannon, *Governor Reagan*: 213.
39. "Reagan Affirms Anti-Abortion Stand," *New York Times*, February 8, 1976; Ronald Reagan to Kenneth Fisher, circa late 1970s, reprinted in *Reagan: A Life in Letters*, New York, 2003: 363.
40. Reagan to Fisher, reprinted in *Reagan: A Life in Letters*: 167.
41. Charles D. Hobbs, "How Ronald Reagan Governed California," *National Review*, January 17, 1975: 39.
42. Allan H. Ryskind, "Reagan's Greatest Success as Governor," *Human Events*, June 28, 2004: 16.
43. "The Story of Ronald Reagan: Governor of Nation's Biggest State," *U.S. News & World Report*, January 2, 1967: 35.
44. Skinner, Anderson, and Anderson, *Reagan: A Life in Letters*: 583.
45. Charles D. Hobbs, "How Ronald Reagan Governed California': 42.
46. Lee Edwards, *Ronald Reagan*: 171.
47. Ibid.; 172.
48. Boyarsky, *The Rise of Ronald Reagan*: 258.
49. Excerpted from an address by Governor Ronald Reagan to the Young Republican National Convention, Omaha, Nebraska, June 23, 1967.
50. Excerpted from an address by Governor Ronald Reagan to the Young Republican National Convention, Omaha, Nebraska, June 23, 1967; Paul O'Neill, "Conservative is the way to sound," *Life*, October 30, 1970: 28; James M. Perry, "When the Skeptics Stopped Laughing," *The National Observer*, July 3, 1967: 1.
51. Cannon, *Governor Reagan*: 386, 389.
52. Daniel J. Balz, "Ronald Reagan," *The Citizen's Guide to the 1976 Presidential Candidates*, 1976: 1.

Chapter 5

1. Ronald Reagan, "We Will Be a City Upon a Hill," Speech before the first Conservative Political Action Conference, January 25, 1974, reagan2020.com/speeches/City_Upon_A_Hill.asp.

2. Helene von Damm, as quoted in Lee Edwards, *Ronald Reagan*: 177.
3. Ibid.: 177–78.
4. Ibid.
5. Rowland Evans and Robert Novak, *The Reagan Revolution*, New York, 1981: 48.
6. David S. Broder, "A Hunch about Reagan," *Washington Post*, July 20, 1975.
7. Gene Tournour, "Reagan Racist Cap in Ring," *Daily World*, November 21, 1975.
8. Edward Walsh, "A Confident Ford Says He Doesn't Care What Reagan Decides," *Washington Post*, March 21, 1976; Gilbert A. Lewthwaite, "Reagan Hints GOP May Lose with Ford," *Baltimore Sun*, March 21, 1976.
9. Cannon, *Governor Reagan*: 424.
10. Ibid.: 425.
11. James R. Dickenson, "Reagan's National Speech Keeps Successful Theme," *Washington Star*, April 1, 1976.
12. "Republican Rumble," *Time*, May 17, 1976: 11; "A President 'in Jeopardy,'" *Newsweek*, May 17, 1976: 22.
13. "My First 100 Days," an interview with Ronald Reagan conducted by Lee Edwards, *Conservative Digest*, August 1976: 5–10.
14. Stephen Hayward, *The Age of Reagan: The Fall of the Old Liberal Order 1964–1980*, Roseville, California, 2001: 475.
15. Morris, *Dutch*: 402.
16. Hayward, *The Age of Reagan*: 479–81.
17. Morris, *Dutch*: 401.
18. "Reagan's Farewell to His Workers," *Washington Post*, August 20, 1976.
19. Frank van der Linden, *The Real Reagan*, New York, 1981: 144.
20. Ibid.: 144.
21. Ronald Reagan to Mrs. Van Voorhis, circa 1976, as reprinted in *Reagan: A Life in Letters*: 277–78.
22. Peter Schweizer, *Reagan's War*, New York, 2002: 93
23. Richard V. Allen, "Reagan's Early Call: Win Cold War," *Human Events*, October 27, 2003: 8.
24. Ibid.
25. Hayward, *The Age of Reagan*: 616.

26. Kiron K. Skinner, Annelise Anderson, Martin Anderson, *Reagan in His Own Hand*, New York, 2001: xxii.

27. Ibid.: 30–31.

28. Ibid.: 370–73.

29. Ibid.: 380, 359.

30. Ronald Reagan to Ms. Jamie Harrison, reprinted in *Reagan: A Life in Letters*, New York, 2003: 270–71.

31. Austin Ranney, *The American Elections of 1980*, Washington, D.C., 1981: 31.

32. *Human Events*, August 25, 1979: 1.

33. "Reagan: Leading Contender, But Age Looms," *U.S. News & World Report*, May 7, 1979: 54–56.

34. Cannon, *Governor Reagan*: 439.

35. Lee Edwards, *Ronald Reagan*: 188.

36. Cannon, *Governor Reagan*: 444.

37. "Reagan: GOP's Front-Runner Starts to Run," *U.S. News & World Report*, November 26, 1979: 48.

38. van der Linden, *The Real Reagan*: 171.

39. Cannon, *Governor Reagan*: 455.

40. Ibid.: 458.

41. Ronald Reagan to Lee Edwards, reprinted in *Reagan: A Life in Letters*: 240.

42. Jeff Greenfield, *The Real Campaign*, New York, 1982: 48.

43. Greenfield, *The Real Campaign*: 48; "Reagan Regains Front-Runner Role," *Human Events,* March 8, 1980: 1, 19.

44. For the David Broder quote, see Lou Cannon, *Governor Reagan*: 462; for Bush quote, see "Reagan's Rousing Return," *Time*, March 10, 1980: 12–16.

45. Cannon, *Governor Reagan*: 450.

46. Mike Wallace, in *Recollections of Reagan: A Portrait of Ronald Reagan*, ed. Peter Hannaford, New York, 1997: 181.

47. Greenfield, *The Real Campaign*: 160.

48. Ibid.: 164.

49. Cannon, *Governor Reagan*: 475.

50. "George Bush on His Role as No. 2," *U.S. News & World Report*, July 28, 1980: 23–24.

51. Cannon, *Governor Reagan*: 476.

52. Ibid.: 477.

53. Cannon, *President Reagan*: 280.
54. "Two for the Show," *Time*, September 22, 1980: 8–9.
55. Cannon, *Governor Reagan*: 492.
56. Greenfield, *The Real Campaign*: 235–41.
57. Ibid.
58. "Time to Pull Together," *U.S. News & World Report*, November 10, 1980: 100ff.
59. Lee Edwards, *Ronald Reagan*: 232; Greenfield, *The Real Campaign*: 244–45.
60. Cannon, *President Reagan*: 300.
61. Interview of Ronald Reagan by Dan Blackburn, NBC Radio, October 31, 1980, as quoted in Cannon, *Governor Reagan*: 83.
62. "Start of a New Era," *U.S. News & World Report*, November 17, 1980: 21–66, 90–110; "That Winning Smile," *Time*, November 17, 1980: 20–24ff: "Election Special," *Newsweek*, November 17, 1980: 27-34ff.
63. Cannon, *Governor Reagan*: 177; Richard J. Whalen, "Peach-Pit Conservative or Closet Moderate?" *New York Times Sunday Magazine*, May 22, 1976: 52.

Chapter 6

1. "A Modest Program," *Wall Street Journal*, September 22, 1980.
2. Martin Anderson, *Revolution*, San Diego, 1988: 232.
3. Edwin Meese III, *With Reagan*, Washington, D.C., 1992: 121.
4. "RWR's Own New Deal," *Newsweek*, March 2, 1981.
5. All figures are taken from William A. Niskanen and Stephen Moore, "Supply-Side Tax Cuts and the Truth about the Reagan Economic Record," *Policy Analysis*, October 22, 1996, published by the Cato Institute.
6. Ronald Reagan to Reuben Betancourt, December 1, 1981, as reprinted in *Reagan: A Life in Letters*: 304.
7. Thomas Sowell, "Achievements and Judgments," *Washington Times*, June 10, 2004.
8. "President Reagan Inaugural Address," *New York Times*, January 21, 1981.
9. Reagan, *An American Life*: 196–97.
10. Ibid.: 316.

11. Kevin R. Hopkins, "Social Welfare Policy: A Failure of Vision," in ed. David Boaz, *Assessing the Reagan Years*, Washington, D.C., 1989: 211.

12. Donald Devine, *Reagan's Terrible Swift Sword: An Insider's Story of Abuse and Reform within the Federal Bureaucracy*, Ottawa, Illinois, 1991: 1.

13. Ron Haskin and Representative Hank Brown, "A Billion Here, A Billion There," *Policy Review,* Summer 1989: 22–28.

14. Ronald Reagan, "A Time for Choosing," reprinted in *Speaking My Mind*: 31.

15. Cannon, *President Reagan*: 247.

16. Ibid.: 179.

17. Reagan, *An American Life*: 335.

18. Ronald Reagan to Edward H. Sims, March 22, 1982, as reprinted in *Reagan: A Life in Letters*: 311.

19. Stephen Moore, "Who Really Balanced the Budget?" *The American Enterprise,* November-December 1997: 52.

20. D'Souza, *Ronald Reagan*: 104.

21. Ibid.

22. Laurence I. Barrett, *Gambling with History: Ronald Reagan in the White House*, Garden City, New York, 1983: 80.

23. D'Souza, *Ronald Reagan*: 93.

24. D'Souza, *Ronald Reagan*: 89; Lee Edwards, *The Power of Ideas: The Heritage Foundation at 25 Years,* Ottawa, Illinois, 1997: 55.

25. Paul E. Peterson and Mark Rom, "Lower Taxes, More Spending and Budget Deficits," in *The Reagan Legacy: Promise and Performance*, ed. Charles O. Jones, Chatham, New Jersey, 1988: 219–20.

26. Lee Edwards, *Ronald Reagan*: 263; Morris, *Dutch*: 431.

27. Lee Edwards, *Ronald Reagan*: 265.

28. Morris, *Dutch*: 431.

29. Ibid.: 432.

30. Michael Deaver, *A Different Drummer*, New York, 2002: 145–47.

31. Lee Edwards, *Ronald Reagan*: 270.

32. See my entry in *Recollections of Reagan*, edited by Peter Hannaford, New York, 1997: 52–53.

33. *Recollections of Reagan: A Portrait of Ronald Reagan*: xiii.

34. Meese, *With Reagan*: 147.

35. Nofziger, *Nofziger*: 285.
36. "Reagan's State of the Union Address," reprinted in *Reagan: The Next Four Years*, Washington, D.C., 1985: 153.
37. Lee Edwards, *Freedom's College: The History of Grove City College*, Washington, D.C., 2000: 229; Lou Cannon, *President Reagan*: 730–31.
38. Robert Rector and Michael Sanera, eds., *Steering the Elephant: How Washington Works*, New York, 1987: 338.
39. Peter Schweizer, *Reagan's War*, New York, 2002: 139–40.
40. *Reagan: A Life in Letters*: 311.
41. Peter J. Ferrara, "What Really Happened in the 1980s?" *Issues '94: The Candidate's Briefing Book*, Washington, D.C., 1994: 16–17; Richard B. McKenzie, *What Went Right in the 1980s*, San Francisco, 1994: 1.
42. David M. O'Brien, "The Reagan Judges: His Most Enduring Legacy?" in *The Reagan Legacy*: 60–61.
43. O'Brien, "The Reagan Judges: His Most Enduring Legacy?": 62. For Sheldon Goldman quote, see Cannon, *President Reagan*: 721.
44. "Reagan Picks Bork, Sparks Liberal Uproar," *Washington Times*, July 2, 1987.
45. Cannon, *President Reagan*: 807.
46. Ibid.: 802.
47. William J. Bennett to the author, September 3, 1997.
48. Peter J. Ferrara, "The Politics of Substance," in *Issues '94*, Washington, D.C., 1994: 1.

Chapter 7

1. "Start of the Reagan Era," *U.S. News & World Report*, January 26, 1981: 18–20; Reagan, *An American Life*: 267.
2. Peter Schweizer, *Victory: The Reagan Administration's Secret Strategy That Hastened the Collapse of the Soviet Union*, New York, 1994: xiv.
3. Peter Schweizer, *Reagan's War*, New York, 2002: 144.
4. Ibid.: 143.
5. Cannon, *President Reagan*: 314–15.
6. "Ronald Reagan's Flower Power," *New York Times*, June 9, 1982.
7. Schweizer, *Victory*: xv.
8. Schweizer, *Reagan's War*: 141.

9. Ibid.: 156.

10. Schweizer, *Victory*: 126.

11. Ibid.: 131.

12. Charles Krauthammer, "The Reagan Doctrine," *Time*, April 1, 1985: 54.

13. In a central position on Reagan's desk in the Oval Office was the sign: "There is no limit to what a man can do or where he can go if he doesn't mind who gets the credit." See Dinesh D'Souza, *Ronald Reagan*: 30.

14. Schweizer, *Reagan's War*: 256.

15. Reagan, *An American Life*: 479.

16. Ibid.: 568–71; Vaclav Havel, "Words on Words," *New York Review of Books*, January 18, 1990: 58; D'Souza, *Ronald Reagan*: 135.

17. Charles Krauthammer, "Reluctant Cold Warriors," *Washington Post*, November 12, 1999; for Buckley quote, see Kengor, *God and Ronald Reagan*: 253–54. For "just war" analogy, see page 269 of Kengor's book.

18. "Goliath in Grenada," *New York Times*, October 30, 1983; Constantine Menges, *Inside the National Security Council*, New York, 1988: 89.

19. Menges, *Inside the National Security Council*: 158.

20. Andrew E. Busch and Elizabeth Edwards Spalding, "1983," *Policy Review*, Fall 1993: 72.

21. Busch and Edwards Spalding, "1983": 72.

22. Cannon, *President Reagan*: 739; Geoffrey Smith, *Reagan and Thatcher*, New York, 1991: 146.

23. Joel Brinkley, "Is Reagan Now Less Hard on Communism?" *New York Times*, December 20, 1987.

24. As told by former Governor Pete Wilson in *Recollections of Reagan*: 198.

25. Caspar W. Weinberger, *Fighting for Peace*, New York, 1990: 293–94; Weinberger, "U.S. Defense Strategy," in *The Reagan Foreign Policy*, ed., William G. Hyland, New York, 1987: 185.

26. Edward Teller in *Recollections of Reagan*: 169; D'Souza, *Ronald Reagan*: 174.

27. Daniel O. Graham, *Confessions of a Cold Warrior*, Fairfax, Virginia, 1995: 103.

28. Cannon, *President Reagan*: 320.

29. George A. Keyworth, interview, September 28, 1987, Oral History Project, Ronald Reagan Presidential Library, Simi Valley, California.
30. *New York Times* editorial, March 27, 1983.
31. Graham, *Confessions of a Cold Warrior*: 165.
32. Schweizer, *Reagan's War*: 152; Graham, *Confessions*: 153.
33. Richard Gid Powers, *Not without Honor: The History of American Anti-Communism*, New York, 1995: 429.
34. Schweizer, *Reagan's War*: 180; Carl Bernstein, "The Holy Alliance," *Time*, February 24, 1992: 28–35; Lech Walesa, *Proceedings of "The Failure of Communism: The Western Response,"* an international conference sponsored by Radio Free Europe/Radio Liberty, November 15, 1989: 47.
35. Schweizer, *Reagan's War*: 188.
36. Peter B. Levy, *Encyclopedia of the Reagan-Bush Years*. Westport, Connecticut, 1996: 47.
37. Reagan, *An American Life*: 680–83.
38. Peter Robinson, "Tearing Down That Wall," *Weekly Standard*, June 23, 1997: 8.
39. Robinson, "Tearing Down That Wall": 708.
40. Alexis de Tocqueville, *The Old Regime and the Revolution*, New York, 1856: 214.
41. Reagan, *An American Life*: 713–14.
42. Cannon, *President Reagan*: 786.
43. Reagan, *An American Life*: 715.
44. Cannon, *President Reagan*: 656, 661.
45. Reagan, *An American Life*: 513.
46. Ronald Reagan, an address to the nation, March 4, 1987. Reagan, *A Life in Letters*: 475.
47. Quoted in James Schlesinger, "Reykjavik and Revelations: A Turn of the Tide?" in *America and the World 1986*, ed. William G. Hyland. New York, 1987: 441; Ronald Reagan to Laurence W. Beilenson, December 10, 1986, *Reagan: A Life in Letters*: 471.
48. Meese, *With Reagan*: 271.
49. Powers, *Not without Honor*: 411.
50. Ibid.
51. Meese, *With Reagan*: 286.
52. *Reagan: A Life in Letters*, Skinner, Anderson and Anderson: 469; Constantine Menges, *Inside the National Security Council*: 317.

53. Select Committee of the House and Senate, *Report of the Congressional Committees Investigating the Iran-Contra Affair.* Washington, D.C., 1987: 21, 437–38.
54. Cannon, *President Reagan*: 657–58.
55. Ibid.: 831.
56. Spencer Rich, "For Reagan, the Last Radio Show," *Washington Post*, January 15, 1989.
57. *Reagan: The Next Four Years.* Washington, D.C., 1984: 15.
58. Cannon, *President Reagan*: 549.
59. Ibid.: 548.
60. Ibid.: 550.
61. Michael A. Ledeen, "Reagan Seen Plain," June 6, 2004, National Review Online.
62. "Ronald Reagan from the People's Perspective: A Gallup Poll Review," June 7, 2004, news release distributed by the Gallup Organization; also see Lou Cannon, *President Reagan*: xi.
63. See the June 6, 2004, Gallup review.
64. James Taranto, "Washington Remembers Reagan," June 11, 2004, Opinion Journal, distributed by the *Wall Street Journal*.
65. Walter Williams, *Reaganism and the Death of Representative Democracy.* Washington, D.C., 2003: 15.
66. W. Elliot Brownlee and Hugh David Graham, eds., *The Reagan Presidency: Pragmatic Conservatism and Its Legacies.* Lawrence, Kansas, 2003: 5, 368–71.
67. As quoted in a review of *Cold War Triumphalism after the Fall of Communism*, New York, 2004, by Harvey Klehr. *Washington Times*, June 20, 2004.
68. James Hershberg, "Just Who Did Smash Communism?" *Washington Post*, June 27, 2004.
69. Cannon, *President Reagan*: 748.
70. Robert Dallek, *Ronald Reagan: The Politics of Symbolism (With a New Preface)*, Cambridge, Massachusetts, 2000: xiii.
71. Kengor, "Reagan among the Professors," www.policyreview.org/dec99/kengor_print.html.
72. Garry Wills, *Reagan's America*, London, 1988: 361, 377.
73. Haynes Johnson, *Sleepwalking through History: America in the Reagan Years*, New York, 2003: 12.
74. "Reagan Toppled Foes who Took Him Lightly," *USA Today*, June 11, 2004.

75. Garry Wills, *Reagan's America: Innocents at Home*, New York, 2000: xviii.
76. Morris, *Dutch*: 640.
77. Morris, "The Unknowable," *New Yorker*, June 28, 2004.
78. Reagan, *Speaking My Mind*: 412.
79. Anthony Lewis, "What Reagan Wrought," *New York Times*, June 21, 1984.
80. Benjamin Friedman, *Day of Reckoning: The Consequences of American Economic Policy Under Reagan and After*, New York, 1988: 24; Paul Krugman, *The Age of Diminished Expectations: U.S. Economic Policy in the 1990s*, Cambridge, 1990: 23.
81. Tom Shales, "'The Reagans': Not Quite a Hatchet Job," *Washington Post*, November 30, 2003; Cannon, *President Reagan*: 733.
82. Robert Novak, "Reagan as Cartoon Character," *Washington Post*, December 4, 2003; Tom Shales, "'The Reagans'": A Low Blow for Gipper," *Washington Post*, November 30, 2003.
83. Philip Kennicott, "Reagan's Legacy, Where 'Angels' Dare to Tread, *Washington Post*, December 21, 2003.
84. L. Brent Bozell III, "New Myths on Reagan's Record," June 16, 2004, Media Research Center.
85. Ronald Reagan, Farewell Address to the Nation, January 11, 1989.

Chapter 8

1. Andrew E. Busch, *Ronald Reagan and the Politics of Freedom*, Lanham, Maryland, 2001: 253–54.
2. William A. Niskanen and Stephen Moore, "Supply-Side Tax Cuts and the Truth about the Reagan Economic Record": 31; Dinesh D'Souza, *Ronald Reagan*: 113.
3. Paul Craig Roberts, "Capitalist Revolution," *The American Conservative*, July 5, 2004: 13–14.
4. Roberts, "Capitalist Revolution": 13–14.
5. Cannon, *President Reagan*: 759.
6. Lawrence Kudlow, "Reaganomics," *National Review*, June 28, 2004: 28–29.
7. Michael Barone, "He Leaves a Surprisingly Grand Legacy," *U.S. News and World Report*, June 2004: 78.
8. Kiron Skinner, "Reagan's Plan," June 11, 2004, distributed by the American Enterprise Institute.

9. Skinner, "Reagan's Plan."

10. Richard Perle, "How They Misjudged the Reagan I Knew," June 8, 2004, distributed by the American Enterprise Institute.

11. Ken Adelman, "The Real Reagan," *Wall Street Journal*, June 9, 2004.

12. Natan Sharansky, "Afraid of the Truth," *Washington Post*, October 12, 2000.

13. Lech Walesa, "Remembering Reagan," reprinted in *Wall Street Journal*, June 14, 2004.

14. Leon Aron, "How Reagan Made Soviet Society Face Its Failures," June 10, 2004, posted by the American Enterprise Institute.

15. Ibid.

16. Cannon, *President Reagan*: 18; Anne Reilly Dowd, "What Managers Can Learn from President Reagan," *Fortune*, September 15, 1986.

17. David Frum, "Dutch: Spine of Steel Wrapped in Geniality," *National Post* (Canada), June 7, 2004.

18. Reagan, *An American Life*: 380, 384.

19. Morris, *Dutch*: 529–31.

20. Ibid.: 662.

21. Michael Deaver with Mickey Herskowitz, *Behind the Scenes*, New York, 1987: 39.

22. Cannon, *President Reagan*: 446.

23. Richard Neustadt, *Presidential Power*, New York, 1976: 10. Also see all of chapter 3, "The Power to Persuade."

24. Peter Schweizer, *Reagan's War*: 279.

25. Cannon, *President Reagan*: xiv.

26. Morris, *Dutch*: 668. See pages 665–66 of *Dutch* for the full text of the letter.

27. *Reagan: A Life in Letters*: 834.

28. Ibid.: 431.

29. Ibid.: 433.

30. Cannon, *President Reagan*: 95–96.

31. D'Souza, *Ronald Reagan*: 186.

32. Morris, *Dutch*: 665–66.

33. Schweizer, *Reagan's War*: 284

34. Reagan, *An American Life*: 335.

35. Newt Gingrich, "The Heir to FDR," *The Hill*, June 8, 2004.

36. Ronald Reagan, *Abortion and the Conscience of the Nation*, Nashville, Tennesseee, 1984: 11, 13.

37. "The Great Rejuvenator: Ronald Reagan's Greatest Speeches," ed. Adam Meyerson, *Policy Review*, Spring 1989: 7.

38. Marilyn Berger, "Reagan Dies at 93," *New York Times*, June 6, 2004.

39. Larry Elder, "Did Reagan 'Torture' Blacks?" *Human Events*, June 21, 2004.

40. T. R. Reid, "A Flirtation with Greed, but Bedrock Beliefs Stay Solid," *Washington Post*, December 14, 1989.

41. Reagan, *Speaking My Mind*: 118.

42. Reagan, *An American Life*: 311.

43. *Reagan: A Life in Letters*: 83.

44. Peter J. Wallison, "Remembering Reagan," *AEI Newsletter*, July 2004. Wallison, who served as counsel to the president during two difficult years—1986–1987—has written an excellent book about the experience, *Ronald Reagan: The Power of Conviction and the Success of His Presidency*, Boulder, Colorado, 2002.

45. Michael Novak, "Our Better Angels," National Review Online, June 7, 2004.

46. Reagan, *Speaking My Mind*: 26 (Goldwater address); 410–18 (farewell address).

47. Matthew J. Franck, "Originalist Thinking," National Review Online, June 9, 2004.

48. Reagan, *Speaking My Mind*: 418.

Index

About the Author

Lee Edwards, Ph.D., is the Distinguished Fellow in Conservative Thought at the Heritage Foundation in Washington, D.C., an adjunct professor of politics at Catholic University of America, and chairman of the Victims of Communism Memorial Foundation. He has published sixteen books, including *The Collapse of Communism* (1999), *The Conservative Revolution: The Movement That Remade America* (1999), and *Goldwater: The Man Who Made a Revolution* (1995).